# Discerning Bipolar Grace

## ~a man at his best dealing with bipolar at its worst~

Rich Melcher

iUniverse, Inc.
New York Bloomington

**Discerning Bipolar Grace**
**~a man at his best dealing with bipolar at its worst~**



*iUniverse books may be ordered through booksellers or by contacting:*

*iUniverse*
*1663 Liberty Drive*
*Bloomington, IN 47403*
*www.iuniverse.com*
*1-800-Authors (1-800-288-4677)*



*ISBN: 978-1-4401-6467-5 (sc)*
*ISBN: 978-1-4401-6468-2 (ebk)*

*Printed in the United States of America*

*iUniverse rev. date: 10/27/2009*

# *Dedication*

The process of creating Discerning Bipolar Grace was made possible by the unwavering sense of hope and encouragement of my wife Sandra. She made it possible for me to persist in the moments of weariness, to tread water in the moments of doubt, and to rejoice in the moments of triumph.

Also, my parents, Lorraine and Bob Melcher, played a key role in editing the book. Without their assistance, this would be a very different book, and a less rich one, at that.

The inspiring comments of my brother, John Melcher, were also very important. I greatly appreciate the love and inspiration of these four people, and to all those in my life who have been a source of encouragement along the way.

# *Rich Melcher*
# *Biography*

Richard Corsair Melcher is the youngest of nine who, after growing up in the peace and calm of rural Minnesota, now calls urban Milwaukee, Wisconsin his home. He began writing poetry and prose in the spring of 1982 and has published three books: Bipolar Balancing Act (2002) and Teachable Moments (2007), and now, Discerning Bipolar Grace, a memoir chronicling the triumphs and struggles of living with bipolar disorder.

Rich is currently completing two other books: Just a Little Somethin' (an enhanced edition of Teachable Moments) and a book of selected poetry entitled Soul In Motion.

Rich's foundation for writing these books stems from 10,000 pages of journal entries written in the past 27 years, which form a basis for his personable, conversational style of writing.

Focusing on urban volunteer ministries in Milwaukee, Rich is a non-crisis phone counselor, a home visit specialist for the St. Vincent de Paul Society, and a meal program assistant at area churches.

Also, Rich and his wife Sandra have recently established an educational consulting business called Authentic Journeys. The main goal of Authentic Journeys is to impact area youth and adults by presenting interactive speeches on various issues surrounding the topic of RESPECT—to bring greater understanding and compassion to the lives of participants.

# *Introduction*

## *Discerning Bipolar Grace* is . . .

. . . the chronicle of a year in the life of the author/speaker Rich Melcher. It was a year (2008) entangled with struggles and joys, extreme highs and moderate lows, peaceful and red-faced moments of anger—all due to the disillusionment and agitation caused by bipolar mania.

The journey has progressed way on down that *winding road of recovery* because of three factors: 1) diligent adherence to a body/mind/spirit recovery program, 2) the support of his wife, family and friends, and 3) the discipline and earnest reflection demanded in writing this book.

Many entries may seem unconnected, yet the process of expressing each, with full honesty and integrity, has led to a stability and excitement for life never thought possible—a true catalyst in promoting the healing process.

Nearly-destroyed relationships have evolved into powerful, close bonds, and a new hope and confidence has been attained—a testament to the power of God and the grace of forgiveness.

The often-emotionally grueling process of creating this memoir has been a *grace* which has led Rich to an all-encompassing reconstruction of a life that had been left dangling in the ruins of bipolar mania.

May it be a blessing to you!

# Chapter 1

## Denial-busting

*We must be true inside—true to ourselves—before we can know a truth that is outside us.*

*Thomas Merton*

October 26, 2008

Three weeks ago, in an unfamiliar apartment, in a scarcely familiar city, I found myself rolling around—confused and sleepless—on a queen-size inflatable bed. Progressively, I began to come to a consciousness that maybe, *just maybe,* I had a problem. I had left my wife, Sandra, in an angry state seven weeks earlier, rushing from Milwaukee, Wisconsin (just north of Chicago) to Grand Rapids, Michigan, which is located directly east of Milwaukee, across Lake Michigan. I had left my primary relationship in the heat and dust of manic flight—a tragic consequence of bipolar disorder.

What is this *bipolar disorder*? Previously called manic-depression, bipolar disorder is a hereditary chemical imbalance in the human brain that can cause dramatic mood fluctuations, and can also lead to cognitive, behavioral, physical and even spiritual abnormalities. All of this can make life difficult and highly unpredictable. Depression had been less common for me since my system, when unbalanced, usually leans toward the manic end of the scale.

"Mania" is, as I see it, exactly the opposite of depression. It is identified by racing thoughts, high energy, over-creativity, over-blown symbolizing (where everything seems to connect for a common purpose), grandiosity and a general belief that everything one does is right. In its advanced stages, self-righteous and self-justifying behaviors prevail! Along with making life unmanageable for the one in mania, it can also make life hell for those who love and/or live with a person experiencing these symptoms.

This was the case for my wife Sandra. Just before our wedding on October 6, 2007, I had been misguided by the psychiatrist whose care I was under. He took me off ALL of my Lithium, my "wonder drug"—a mood stabilizer I'd been taking since 1980, when I was first diagnosed with bipolar. My advice as a *non-doctor*? Never completely stop someone's major medication because there is an *indication* that there *may be* trouble in the future! This doctor saw a kidney-affecting level rising and, three weeks before our wedding, scratched the Lithium from my medication regimen. This sent me sky-rocketing into a mid-level mania in just a few days! I soon ended up in the hospital in Milwaukee, and was only ½ myself during the wedding. (Well, maybe being only partly present at one's wedding is kind of normal, I guess, but I still won't let that doctor off the hook).

So, on *October 6, 2008*, how did I end up in Grand Rapids, Michigan, rolling around in anguish on an inflatable bed?...denial, stress, lack of sleep and a medication deficiency. Plus, mania has this amazing self-preservation function—well, you know how it is…the old "you're the last one to know it" song and dance! You know, "the fish sees the water last" syndrome! Classic mania hides itself very well. Everyone else knows you have a problem, but you don't have a clue!

Through most of 2008, I was experiencing a very destructive form of mania—what I call "*fully-competent mania*." In my over-friendliness with strangers and impatience and irritation with those I know and love, it probably seemed to others that my competence was questionable. But, in September 2008, I cleaned out our condo of all of my belongings in a single afternoon—while Sandra was at work—loaded a moving van, drove 3 states east, found an affordable apartment, moved all my belongings into the second story flat, hooked up the phone, heat, electricity…THIS is the danger of what I call "fully-competent mania." Great qualities—*highly redeemable qualities*—such as drive, resourcefulness, strength, will-power and foresight . . . all working towards a messed-up goal—solitude at all costs! In the weeks between September 1 and October 6, 2008, I found out quite clearly how to *secure solitude*----just **act crazy**—and EVERYONE will leave you alone! And that's where I ended up—alone, disturbed and sweating on that air mattress.

*We are expected to take our experiences and grow*
*from them—to move beyond*
*the shame of them—*
*to celebrate what they have taught us.*

*Each Day A New Beginning*

After 17 previous hospitalizations, I lay there with a choice . . . do I go in for #18, or just try to ride out this storm? With the waves of anguish crashing over the side of the bed, I decided—in all *humiliating humility*—to call my new Grand Rapids psychiatrist immediately. To my surprise, he placated me, instructing me to double my anti-psychotic medication and go back to bed. I did,…then after 20 minutes of staring at the dimly-lit wall in my shabby apartment—knowing I wasn't going to get to sleep—I realized I was in crisis! I rolled out of bed and quickly called the emergency number to express my urgent situation. This was the beginning of my rebound.

Luckily I had caught the relapse-slide early enough so that I could pack a small bag with essentials and drive myself to the hospital. On the way there, I prayed to Mother Mary to keep me safe, and help me deal with the challenges I was about to experience, as I motored toward the hospital.

*hurricane*

*and so*

*once again*
*the hurricane hit the beach*
*never dreamed I'd see another*
*after all those I've lived thru*

*the trade winds of my mind began to swirl*
*and high waves choking my heart came crashing in*
*on the beach of my soul—my personhood*

*lost*

*once again*
*but this time with a better shelter*
*than past perfect storms*
*do I fight against the raging waves*
*or ride it out sheltered?*
*(knowing that storms "don't last always")*

don't run away
face your demons

*but do I face them by trying to change*
*or understand or let them be?*
*I really don't know*

Amid admittance procedures, on the night of October 6, the intake specialist in Grand Rapids looked shocked when I told her that my new psychiatrist had discouraged me from seeking help at the hospital, having stated that "they won't be able to help you there any more than you can do on your own." She seemed a bit stunned, pausing momentarily, then continued to take down my information. I was so confused that I didn't know *what* to think.

It turned out that this was THE MOST HEALING of the 18 hospitalizations, although it was one of the shortest (7 days). Thanks to proper sleep AND a successful medication adjustment, I healed quickly. But the clincher was having the guts to call Sandra in Milwaukee, that first evening in the hospital, and beginning a dialogue that has led to the best communication, forgiveness and understanding of our year-long marriage! Ironically, I entered the Grand Rapids hospital on the exact date of our first anniversary. Must have been a *God thing*!

Getting eight hours of sleep per night once again—a gift I had not encountered for nearly a year—was a magical wand that swept clear thinking and bodily comfort back into my life. Yet I believe slightly increasing my anti-psychotic medication was equally important in changing my thought processes. Sleep and proper meds—this did the trick! I could concentrate, my sleeping pattern was back in order…and the best part of all, I had *Rich* back—the ME writing here now,…a guy I hadn't seen or experienced consistently for over a year! Imagine that------*ME* again!! A poet come home!

## *creeping out*

*everything is poem*
*when mania creeps out*
*of its damp, dark, mold-covered cave*
*so delighted to see its own reflection*
*in pen & purpose*

*purple passion*
*leaks out of old wineskins*
*of depression and captivity*

*yet poem is not as important as poet*
*the words in volley are mere expressions of self*

*not self*
*itself*

*manic trains of thought with no apparent track*
*wind among the smoky hills of a deeper mind*
*sometimes leaving engineer behind*
*in dust and gravel*

*hope lies in bending of rails*
*to bring the wild iron horse back home again*
*to rest in the station of peace*
*awaiting freight of less weight*

# *Chapter 2*

## *man in mania*

When opening my bank account in Grand Rapids, Michigan, the bank representative innocently asked, "What brought you to Grand Rapids?" My distancing, yet humorous answer—"A U-haul truck!" She said, "Oh, you work for U-haul?" "No. I came here in a U-haul truck. I left my wife—we're getting a divorce."

Pretty forward language with someone I had never met before. Point of distinction— nearly always, when I have been manic, I have made personal information public, and *withheld* personal information from my closest ones…such as the afternoon of my abrupt departure to Michigan, in late August, 2008. I had left Sandra on three previous occasions prior to my running off to Grand Rapids, but this time I had set up a contingency…"If she opens up and talks about our argument last night, I will consider NOT leaving…but if she doesn't mention it, I'm outa here!" She didn't. And I was. My pride was so built up that I refused to tell her of my need to talk about the night before and felt justified in leaving when she couldn't read my mind.

But this was at the tail end of a year-long (2008) battle for my mental health that started in September '07 when my meds were maladjusted. Although I have 28 years of experience with bipolar of which I could write, I have chosen to focus on 2008 because the main and most crucial difference was that it involved nearly crippling the relationship between Sandra and me. The illness threatened to take from me my step-children and step-grandchildren, my family of origin, and could have severely and negatively transformed Sandra's life—and left us estranged! This episode was a relationship-killer.

One factor I hadn't considered until I was safely back in Milwaukee in late October 2008 was that I was not only abandoning my wife, Sandra, but my entire "step-family." My self-image was so bent out of shape that I was willing to give up a great life…and for what? Nothing!… but solitude and loneliness, not to mention the broken hearts I had strewn along the roadside as I blew through Chicago in my U-haul, on the way to "a new wonderful life" in Michigan.

All of this drama and distraction was unnecessary—except, seemingly, to a man who was ill, and whose illness was screaming at him to escape. Yet ultimately, I was escaping from MYSELF and my past, and moving toward a future so unsure that I could do nothing but run squarely into it! I was on a dead end course down the road to disaster, and the only thing that could save me was a miracle—the miracle of waking up…of getting low enough to fly under the radar of manic delusion and break the denial barrier that kept me trapped.

## *tiger in my pocket*

*wouldn't you know*
*that the very pain and disillusionment I thought was long gone*
*rests wearily…anxiously…even comfortably…*
*in a beast-caging pocket stitched into each garment of my life*
*~ be it physical, emotional, intellectual or spiritual ~*
*affecting every experience—day and night . . .*
*what is this creature, you wonder?*
*I have a tiger . . . a tiger in my pocket*

I was beginning to be able to name the face of the tiger back in 1989 while fulfilling my one and only stay at a state hospital, in Minnesota. I had found myself in a manic furor and tore up my parents' home to an extent that proved I was a danger to myself—and possibly to them. In the hospital, a counselor suggested that I write down the symptoms that appear when I become manic. I became inspired and spent many days writing down the details, and called them my "manic clues." Here are a number of them:

Manic Clues

1. Sense of urgency
2. Heightened energy
3. Sleeping less than 5 hours
4. Quick to anger
5. "Don't get in my way" attitude
6. Tunnel vision
7. Driving faster/recklessly
8. Destructive to relationships, and things
9. Feel called to the "extreme extraordinary"
10. Obsession with writing
11. Euphoric, no matter what happens
12. Grandiosity
13. Racing thoughts
14. Quitting my job without seeing financial consequences
15. Over-active, over-creative, over-EVERYTHING
16. Trying to prove self
17. Impulsive over-spending
18. Unaware of others' reactions to one's behavior
19. Verbally/physically aggressive
20. **Unaware of all of the above; not able to see how one is affecting others and the social environment**

I have gone through stages where I was very aware of these manic clues, yet I had not been in tune with them in the past few years. Why? I guess sometimes we forget what can help us the most. I had forgotten.

Of the eight manic episodes I have encountered, 2008's was the longest and the strangest. Ever since my previous med maladjustment, my moods had shifted from a hidden depression to an over-creative, insomnia-ridden mania—kind of a "Mr. Nice Guy / Mr. Jerk," phenomenon... back & forth, over and over. It was horrendous, disturbing and costly—emotionally, financially and relationally. I remember how I had scoffed at my oldest brother John's statement to Sandra that I was "out of control." I can hear it now, my muffled laughter that..."*someone could think of <u>me</u> as being out of control?* I know exactly what I'm doing," I had thought at the time.

Funny how I can recall that period with a healthy detachment and distance—a gift given to me by what I refer to as "*the Observer*." It's like having a 24-hour video camera recording life's happenings—no judgments, no opinions, no involvement—merely recording. This *Observer* is not really a "conscience," since that implies a judgment of thought and behavior. Rather it just watches and listens—and knows exactly the emotional and physical ramifications that occur at the time. But it doesn't expose these to the conscious manic self.

So, at <u>this</u> moment, I can *feel* how I felt when my brother said I was *out of control*, and *see* what I did about it, because all the information had been recorded by my Observer. When I had become extremely angry with Sandra in August, I can (only now) see the fearful look on her face that had no meaning then. And by not "seeing it" then, I made some major miscalculations and veered onto a divergent path. Yes, even one missed nonverbal cue can make a <u>big</u> difference!

My *Observer*, this mysterious part of the human memory, allows me to see, now, how my manic episode created so much havoc, grief and pain. I now see and feel what I'd been warned about—that manic episodes can get worse in time,...and at age 47—after the 2008 debacle—I really don't ever want to have a relapse again! In fact, <u>I will do anything needed</u> to make sure it doesn't happen again, including chronicling my experiences here to share my story with you, in order to move you toward more awareness, understanding, and acceptance of bipolar. I thank God for my ability to write—prose and poetry—that gives me the outlet and concentrated efforts that allow sanity to be my friend.

In the silence of my mind, the *Observer* watched, listened to and documented this distorted journey. In patient silence, the *Observer* waited for me to come back.

*s i l e n c e*

*no sighs or violence*
*stillness absolute*
*not a breeze whispering through complaisant pine*
*nor gently folding lap on rocky shore*
*lonely hawk's absent plea cheats the cool night air*
*and cricket chirp choir rests voiceless*
*ear grasping the nothingness*
*(loudest sound never heard)*

*to be motionless*
*noiseless*
*loud as running sap*
*or ant scurrying*
*eardrums crying for lack of a drummer*

*once silence is heard*
*the beat*
*the melody*
*the rhythm*
*the tone*
*it leaves its impression forever*

*(the trees will know you then)*

# *Chapter 3*

## *new beginnings*

"There will be two young children in the White House come January..." were the words I remember hearing as NBC's Brian Williams announced that Barack Obama would be our next president. Not a shock, but a joy, to hear this uplifting and hope-filled news.

Seems like yesterday evening that Sandra and I were at a party (actually in late August of 2008) when Sarah Palin had been introduced as John McCain's running mate. My immediate reaction? "They just lost the election!" A token woman to off-set Hillary Clinton, someone McCain didn't even really *know*...it just seemed like one more gimmick for the McCain campaign. Sandra came through the room, and, seeing this woman on TV with really nice glasses, thought "Oh, it's a new LensCrafters commercial." Humorous assumption, but it might as well have been a LensCrafters commercial.

I had no idea, at that moment, that two days later I'd be leaving Sandra—once more—"for good"...which had happened just over two weeks earlier. So when did this "need for freedom" arise? Where did this desire to leave Sandra begin? This doesn't happen often, but I can name the date—and the time...10:30 a.m., Saturday, July 19, 2008. How the heck could I know this?

This was the moment I called Sandra from Chicago to weigh in on my feelings of disappointment and disillusionment about a "life coach" training program I was deeply invested in—intellectually, scholastically, emotionally and financially. (A life coach is someone who helps you visualize your strengths, goals and dreams—then assists in helping you make them become a reality). This was to be, at age 46, my dream job. I'd been a janitor, teacher's aide, customer service representative, group home care attendant,…but I'd never been a *professional.* Thinking about it, would five weekend life coach seminars, towing a heavy price tag, make me a "professional"? The trainers made it <u>seem</u> that way…a perception with which I readily and fully "bought into."

As this seminar unfolded, I came to the awareness that these coaching techniques were dysfunctional. Throughout the previous three weekend seminars, the trainers had demeaned counseling as being only for *sick people,* yet it seemed like they were attempting to teach *counseling* techniques, of some sort, at this fourth seminar. As coaching trainees, we were taught how to—in my view—bring clients into their "dark side," fumble around with them, then somehow bring them back out all squeaky clean. I found this to be not only odd, but potentially dangerous, and even repulsive. I began to think, "If you lead someone down into a coal mine, then turn off the light, who is going to lead them back out?" Since I'd been in counseling, off and on, for nearly 30 years, I recognized the faulty and ill-informed instruction immediately.

Following the 10:30 a.m. call to Sandra, in which we discussed how the seminar was progressing (or regressing), I reluctantly went back into the lion's den (classroom). After a few minutes of further "instruction," I confronted the instructors—head-on—about how I saw the training as deficient and possibly even destructive. I pointed out that I'd been in counseling for numerous years and that I could see a huge difference between this type of "coaching" and the therapy I had been receiving. My counseling sessions had been much more like the training in the previous seminars which promoted open-ended questions and excellent listening skills. But this? This seemed like a pseudo-crash-testing exercise that appeared unnecessary, at best! Counseling had been demonized throughout the first three weekends—that had been made clear—but what were we to think of <u>this</u>?

I also pointed out that my therapists were trained, competent, experienced professionals, and they (the coaching trainers) were not. Pretty "in-your-face," but I felt it had to be said. The trainers were so stymied that they bumbled, fumbled and finally mumbled something about the coach training organization having a *"high-level of standards"* and that they were "*the best in the field*"—not a word of which I bought.

(This story does lead to how I ended up abandoning my wife, but first I must tell you that)...I wasn't concerned about my own coaching abilities, having been trained as a volunteer mental health support counselor, and having so much experience being counseled myself. But I was concerned that some of my fellow coaching students may find themselves in some negative situations for which they might be totally unprepared. They could possibly encounter clients who have various emotional disorders, and the techniques we were learning might be explosive! Also, I was in disbelief that I would be expected, as a coach, to use these faulty techniques on trusting clients. I couldn't stomach that!

After I aired my comments, we split into pairs, and my coaching partner was to "do some coaching" using these slanted techniques... the main idea being to "bring 'em down the hole!" I was so angry and disillusioned that my coaching partner had a difficult time coaching me. Yet when I coached her, I ignored the day's new precepts and just listened compassionately, offered a few insights, and got her on her way—using the helpful techniques from the three previous seminars.

Then at lunchtime—having had enough—I went up to my hotel room, packed, enjoyed lunch with a colleague, and left the Chicago seminar for good, heading north to Milwaukee. I drove toward home with mixed emotions of relief and disappointment. With two weekend conferences and the certification process remaining, I quit the program. I felt forced to quit on my dream because of the deep philosophical and moral discrepancies—sighting contradictions between *my* vision of coaching and the coach training program's vision.

Here's where the "need to leave Sandra" factor came in. The *pay-off* for quitting the program was that, because I left the program, I was able to enjoy my step-granddaughter's baptism the next day. Tragically, this set up the pattern for three future "desertions"…the pattern?... suspicion, criticism, anger, disillusionment, packing in secret, and abruptly disconnecting. My retreat from the coach training program established a destructive pattern in my psyche. Abandonment of Sandra soon became the order of the day, occurring on August 8, August 31 and September 15, 2008…for some unknown reason, all about two weeks apart. Absolute shock to Sandra every time! But the last time, on September 15th, it seemed to be a relief to "have it over with," she told me later.

Why had the life coaching debacle been such a turning point? Well, think about it...I lost my dream, then gained the joy of an unexpected experience (my step-granddaughter's baptism)... and there's a recipe for "slash, trash & earn" . . . I had *slashed* the tires on a "misguided" coaching program, *trashed* my life-dream of becoming a coach, and then *earned* an unexpected pay-off—(the baptism). Perfect pattern for future disasters! And THAT it was!

It was so devastating that I believe my bipolar came out of the closet to *defend me*—in an unwelcomed manner I call "encased in lead and slammed over the head." This is where…I tend to encounter "my truth," (no matter how small & even insignificant—or hugely significant) and use abrupt and/or offensive interpersonal skills to get my point across. Although this was not my stance or behavior at the coaching seminar, it had been a frequent style of communicating ever since the big med screw-up in September 2007, mentioned earlier, that shifted my mental health form stable to wobbly.

This form of "wobbly," most noticeable to Sandra, was a sort of "Dr. Jekyll and Mr. Hyde" phenomenon where, with no apparent provocation, my personality would shift from "Mr. Nice Guy" to "Mr. Jerk"—instantly. Utterly confusing, disturbing and frightening for her— strangely empowering, self-determining and freeing for me. Only one thing………….it wasn't "ME!"...it wasn't *Rich*—the healthy me! It was an "alter-ego" in which the illness "rented retail space" and ruled my psyche—my thoughts, feelings and actions at those times of stress and lost-ness.

After 29 years of experience with bipolar, and MANY MANY occasions (as I look back) where this alter-ego has come out of hiding, I only recently detected his existence. So I named him. I call this extreme manic alter-ego "***Sham***." He is, in all actuality (as far as I can tell) a different entity than the person who is writing right now. I have come to understand that Sham is the unleashed expression of years of unexpressed feelings: Anger, fear, disappointment, frustration, humiliation, self-pity—all rolled up into a rolling lead ball, spinning down and crushing anything in his way! He's a bundle of the worst parts of me, exposed and in action.

Allow me to describe *Sham* by using a computer analogy…when I am "normal," I enjoy *Rich*-software (the healthy me) installed in the computer of my mind. When I become overwhelmed by bipolar mania, the software gets replaced with a *Sham*-program...different thoughts, different feelings, different behaviors. During all of 2008, my software was clicking in and out of separate *Rich* and *Sham* programs, often instantly and seemingly unprovoked! By late August, *Sham* had taken over completely. The illness was ruling my mind—and my actions!

It is like *Rich* is the pilot of the plane on my life's journey, and *Sham* drags *Rich* behind the pilot's seat and binds and gags him. *Rich* can still see and hear the goings-on, but can do little or nothing about it. *Sham* takes over the cockpit.

## *monster in the veins*

*who would have known*
*this amiable, peaceful guy*
*could hurl daggers*
*of devastating destruction*
*mostly at the ones he knows and loves best*

*who is this person inside a person?*
*who is the monster in the veins?*
*blood channeled frothy & rich, in misguided pleasantries to the brain*
*bashing job, place, people . . . while dashing dreams in the rocks of*

*some sort of need for FREEDOM*
*freedom from what?!*
*(probably from his own insanity!)*

*unyielding relentless forceful focused*
*creativity insightful*
*(all treasured attributes used upside-down & inside-out)*

*KNOWING TO BE RIGHT*

*in the dusty disgust of broken-down bridges*
*and feelings hurt and bleeding -*
*who can trust, again*
*the man who "comes to"*
*in the middle of the battle ground*
*seemingly* **himself** *again*
*having been this other self—this t h i n g?*

*may seem devastating and confusing to the victims*
*but who is the greatest victim of this "bad-blood bath"—*
*this brain imbalance?*
*the one who has been paraded around for over a year in his body*
*with an on-again/off-again monster controlling the wheel*
*'tsbeen no fun to get little sleep and act a fool*
*and not know how to STOP*
*this roller coaster of mood, thought and behavior that*
*has brought so much pain and confusion*

*roller coaster now stopped with meds and snooze,*
*maybe the monster will go back into its cave—*
*and with health a priority and proactive stance—*
*return "for never"*
*God, only, knows... but now diligence*
*and eagle-eye to symptoms must rule*
*to deplete and control ....... the monster in the veins*

This total take-over lasted from late August 2008 until early October, when I found myself on the verge of relapse, unable to sleep and de-compensating rapidly. So from late August until the moment described in the first line of this book ('confused and sleepless, rolling around on an inflatable bed') the delusion and denial of *Sham's* grip had held me, *Rich*, captive and voiceless. Prayer was practically the only connection I had with the real me, which kept me going in these hard times…along with the prayers of others who love me.

This bipolar illness is strange, deceptive and cunning. It will stop at nothing—even destroying a good man's life and breaking up a fantastic marital union—to get its way! And what did *Sham* want? He seemed to only want one thing…*freedom*. *Sham* just seemed to want to be left alone, and that's exactly what he got. After *Sham* rejected my wife, my family of origin, my step-family, my church family and other friends, he moved to Grand Rapids, Michigan. *Sham* had gotten his wish—everyone left him alone. But deep down, the *Rich* inside was miserable, and this became one of the loneliest times of my life.

Below is a poem I wrote, in *Sham*-mode, while in Grand Rapids in September, 2008. In the middle of my *Sham*-driven delusion and dysfunction, you can see the paradoxical seclusion/empowerment theme. Bipolar mania can be very deceitful and elusive.

## *matter*

*when it doesn't really matter*
*no fear caroused*
*no hatred blunted*
*it's a pretty place*
*when no one needs you*
*but hell when nobody*
*wants you*

*and I have both*
*and I have joy*

*and I have it all*
*and, strangely,*
*nothing*

*what I've been searching for all the long*

*home . . . inside . . . and forever*

This faltering alter-ego, *Sham*—this broken part of me—had led me to hurt myself and the ones I love. With God's grace, although the branch was bent, it was not broken, and I am grateful that my life and relationships were spared. With all the heat and pain that this manic episode caused, I am also grateful for the ability to press on, and for the many people in my life who make pressing on possible.

# Chapter 4

## antecedents to an illness

Sitting on a sun-lit, sand-peppered wooden floor, a content eight-year-old listened—once again—to the summer's hit song, "Close To You," by *The Carpenters*. It was July of 1970 and, as the tune meshed with the images it created, a magical event occurred…this young blond-haired Minnesota boy BECAME the boy in the song, the one who *everyone* wanted to be around, the one who was a dream-come-true and, as the song said, the one who "angels put together!"

That day, "***personalization***" was born in me—at age eight. Personalization is where I internalize positive or negative aspects of my surroundings (images, feelings, music) so deeply that I **become** that which I have experienced. I had experienced a piece of Heaven that afternoon in 1970, but, looking back, I'm shocked that it took only 10 years for the gift to become a curse, as I was nearly crushed by my first bipolar depression in 1980.

Being severely depressed is the worst experience I have ever had in my life. It's an ever-present, all-encompassing, self-diminishing shadow that has no boundaries of misery. Here's an image of how much one thinks about their depression when in the midst of it: "Take a large swig of Listerine, swish it around in your mouth a bit, then, don't swallow…just keep it there—for the next 8 hours!! THIS is how much you think about it!" It's nearly impossible to get severe depression off your mind. I've also described depression as having bats hanging down from the inside of your upper rib cage. These are just images...the reality is much worse.

My first depression began to build up around Christmas-time 1979, as I began to have bad dreams and sleeplessness, accompanied by bouts of anxiety. I had been dating the prettiest girl in school (they always say that!) and in late January 1980—which was my senior year in high school—something was coming to a head.

Then, about January 25th or so, it hit me: I was lying in bed, staring at the ceiling and suddenly thought, "I don't think I'm capable of loving my parents…and if I can't love my parents, then how can I love my 8 brothers and sisters?…and if I can't love my brothers and sisters, what about my friends?". . . and on and on and on. Suddenly, all my anxieties had converged, and I fell off the cliff of despair into a hell I had never experienced or dreamed of before. Four sleepless nights, three wretched days of school, two grueling hockey practices and, with one hockey game to go, I found myself on the phone to my oldest brother, John, begging for a solution. He did his best to console me, as the energy drained out of my batteries, but the damage had been done. Sleep finally came, with sheer exhaustion, but the depression had worked its way in and didn't leave for many months.

## *Despondency*

*in a garden of glory*
*where flowers and plants had seemed*
*wondrous and magical, all around*
*how could one be despondent?*

*old habits of thought that*
*imprison and torture*
*in time, untaken & unplanned. . .*
*minutes & hours tick away*

*like sap slowly running*
*and I wonder if I'm crazy for*
*wasting time*

*when will I be free?*

The fiercest torture was that <u>I had no idea I had an illness</u>, or that bipolar even existed! I thought I was just "a bad person" and must deserve this because I had "made bad choices" and was being punished. I didn't see it as a religious persecution, but a moral denouncement of whatever I had done to deserve this. Mystery was an enemy during those days. It was only made clear to me, many months later—after coming through the storm and being diagnosed with bipolar—that my mind had **created** most of these thought patterns and the feelings simply trailed behind them! Then, experiencing the negative feelings, the thoughts often followed this trail of negativity...then more bad feelings, and on and on.

How could this be? How could a chemical deficiency CREATE (or at least mold) thoughts of self-persecution and self-destruction? How could suicide become a viable option in the mind of someone who seemed so happy-go-lucky?

Truth-be-told, this "happiness" had all along held back a melancholy pattern of uneasiness and anxious responses to the world. From early on, I seemed to have encountered a struggle between optimism and pessimism. The depression simply took optimism out of the picture, masking it with fangs and flowing blood so that there seemed to be no light filtering into the dungeon of my imprisoned mind.

Since then, I have learned that chemicals—mainly the transportation and distribution of neurotransmitters between the synapses in the brain—create how we feel. And if these neurotransmitters are malfunctioning, depressive or manic feelings can occur with little or no warning. Bipolar simply makes the emotional ups and downs of life much more contrasted. In other words, the highs and lows seem to be much more dramatic—a sort of oversensitivity to the joys and the pains of life.

## when I feel discouraged

*I feel discouraged*
*when given responsibilities beyond*
*my capabilities and talents*
*and still they bring it on*

*I feel discouraged*
*when my good isn't good enough*
*and I worry that even showin' up*
*through the doors may bring on failure*

*I feel discouraged*
*when I have to feign illness*
*that'll keep me from work*
*because I have fear of being*
*overloaded*

*I feel discouraged*
*when my spiritual life*
*isn't strong enough or deep enough*
*to walk thru a crucible and climb a*
*cross*

*I feel discouraged . . .*
*but I have a God who is BIG ENOUGH*
*to handle my discouragement and I decide*
*to follow in the steps of Christ, in the end, to the end*

That night in late January, 1980, on the phone with my brother, was merely the beginning of the worst 5 months of my life. Along with not knowing I had an illness came the travesty of having to put up a front that I was still the fun, excitable, smart guy that got along with almost everyone. I became an excellent actor, although I found out much later that this disguise was not impervious to the reality that it's nearly impossible to totally hide depression, and my suffering *was* recognized—at least on some level—all along.

*We are what we pretend to be.*

*Kurt Vonnegut, Jr.*

My mother was on the stage, as a school board member, the night of my high school graduation, in June of 1980. I clearly remember the excruciating irony of shaking her hand—being desperately suicidal at the time. Here was the event with which I had looked forward to all those years! I had watched three of my older brothers give graduation speeches in the past four years, and me—ready to "off myself," if I could only find the right time, and the right way. It never came.

What keeps someone so desperate, so tortured, so morbidly emotionally distraught, from "suiciding?" For me, it was my mother. I couldn't hurt her feelings—subject her to such pain. I couldn't! She had been there with me every long-suffering step of the way…including the sleepless nights, my sitting on the couch after school and staring at the ceiling, the dragging myself off to hockey practice. She gave me what I call "Presence"—just being there! She showed the patience, compassion and understanding of a saint, to a multi-struggling youth who was showing only one positive attribute—*perseverance.*

(I talk of suicide quite openly trusting that you understand that suicide is often not a moral dilemma or even an individual choice—but a symptom of a mental illness. It sometimes becomes the "only way" to end such deep and cruel suffering, and, I believe, there should be no judgment placed upon it. It just IS).

*Perseverance…*maybe this is the shining attribute, the golden lining, of a person struggling with suicidal thoughts. Just one more hour—minute—second! I remember how time dragged on and on, with little or no relief. Without knowing it, I was creating a healthy sense of perseverance, which has been an extremely helpful attribute ever since.

*Faith is . . . the ability to carry on with our plans or to be true to our work even though we feel discouraged or tired.*

*Touchstones*

Perseverance has been crucial in my development, but, strikingly, it has been the afore-mentioned *personalization* (the ability to make REAL an experience another may be feeling, at another time, in another location) that has been at the forefront of my existence. Personalization is imagination brought to heart and let loose. It *made me* that wonderful boy on the sunlit Lake Michigan cabin floor in July of 1970, and it *made me* this morose, decrepit-thinking 17-year-old on the verge of suicide in June of 1980.

What is this bipolar? Is this a gift—which allows me to write descriptive poetry and envision lofty goals? Or is it a curse—which creates ugly, dank worlds of depressive thoughts and feelings? Strangely enough, it's both—and every hue in between!

It took until I began working a summer job at my father's construction company in mid-June 1980 for me to pull out of this destructive, depressive dive and head toward brighter skies. With no more "eyes" looking at me in the high school hallways, I found myself working at a job with which I was familiar, having worked there the two previous summers. At the job, I could SEE progress as I put physical effort into this 40-hour per week job. I rarely felt this sense of accomplishment during my high school years. Manual labor can do great things for a person—even a job that others may call "menial work."

But coming out of a bipolar dive meant attaching myself to a rocket—a transition that occurred in only a few weeks. Easing out of depression by early July, I jumped at the opportunity to go on a road trip with seven buddies traveling out West for two weeks. We left

Minneapolis in early August, heading for the western states. My mood lay a bit flat over the Dakotas, but as the mountains of Montana came into view, my mood elevated to the level of the highest peak! Erratic behaviors, (such as demanding the van be stopped so I could get an up-close photo of a bison), began to flow out of me like a mountain stream. Soon, I had seven enemies in the van, hoping I'd get lost at Mount Rushmore, or anywhere between there and Minnesota.

I can look at it now and laugh, for its lunacy, but it wasn't very funny to my friends at the time. I was nearly out of control, donning the cloak of my new-found liveliness—a quality I hadn't seen since before my depression began in late January.

*I had been found*—yes!...(religious reference implied). It was three weeks later, upon applying for admittance into Mankato State University, in southern Minnesota, that I had a spiritual experience that tore the shackles of depression off me for good. I was walking across a campus parking lot with text books in tow, and I told Jesus I was dropping the "suicidal tariff" I had placed on myself many months earlier—that I no longer wanted to kill myself—and asked if the apology I was offering would be accepted. I kid you not,...immediately I felt a warm hand on my left shoulder, as if to say, "Apology accepted...time to move on." There was no one walking by my side...(but there was). Now, I don't know if that was a manic dream-state or what, but it surely seemed real to me at the time.

And so, I was off—off to the races, because my mania revved up even higher from that moment on. I joined the college football team, making a complete fool of myself with my silliness, name-dropping and...roller skating...all over campus—even in the buildings! I was unstoppable! Until my mother came down to my first football game—two weeks before school started.

She had sprained her ankle that Saturday, but decided to drive the 80 miles from Buffalo (my home town) to Mankato anyway. It was her youngest son's first game! Her attitude was "I've gotta go!" She told me, many months later (once I was stable), that when I saw her, I didn't really notice or pay attention to the fact that she was on crutches, nor did I even ask why. I was so full of myself, in my bright purple and gold football uniform…all I wanted was for her to take a picture of me on the field, and for her to see my dorm room.

This strange behavior alerted her to the fact that "something is wrong!" and she insisted I come up to Minneapolis to get a psychiatric evaluation. I bucked it but, in the end, I went. THIS was the beginning of my <u>real</u> healing. I was prescribed Lithium, which is a mood stabilizer, and got back down to Mankato for the start of school.

I tell you all this to show you the fluctuating moods of an unaware, struggling youth who had so much going for him but so little information. The depressive self took the form of a beggar, aching to be free of the chains around his neck:

*in the presence of my*
*s*
*l*
*a*
*n*
*t*
*e*
*d*
*self*
*i see the true me*
*in spite of the tolerant inside*
*i view ugly what-has-not-been-done*
*and all the idle potential*

*i can feel myself slipping into a calm hatred*
*of all this that has been wasted*
*in my presence*
*in my custody*
*all the consuming—and little giving back*
*this throbbing abscess tooth just waiting to implode*
*and smash my self-image into shards*

*of fun-house mirror*

*never to see my true image again*
*dangling-destiny can be a killer*
*all the wait on my shoulders*
*all the wait*

Then the exact opposite came from a "*ME set free*," but spinning into a manic world of kaleidoscope "realities" and an over-activeness that spun the heads of all around me:

*advantage—ME*

*there is no other*
*as I curl my way through masses*
*of shallow, dim personalities*
*it is a wonder that they will ever keep up*
*to my humor and wit*
*clouds fly by*
*but I pay never no mind*
*because I'm free*

*free now*
*to be whomever I want to be*
*don't try 'n' hold me down        I'm free*

This kind of manic "freedom," that occurred the fall after my first depression in 1980, is a dangerous thing, as was the earlier depression that had been so incredibly inhibiting and agonizing. This is a glimpse into bipolar disorder. From doldrums to whirlwind…quite a trip—one I'm doing all I can to avoid experiencing again!

# *Chapter 5*

## *spiritual connections*

*. . . I would seek God, and to God would I commit my cause; who does great things and unsearchable marvelous things without number . . .*

*Job 5:8-9 (Revised Standard Version)*

Over the years, I've done lots of thinking about how to know whether God is leading me, or whether I am being misled by my own spirituality. Upon reading the above Bible quote, the answer finally became clear:

*I need to have God create me, instead of me creating God!*

In late 1986, while in a manic state, I came back to Milwaukee from Minneapolis (where I had returned to after my first hospitalization in Milwaukee) and brought fear and discomfort to some friends with some "spiritually misguided" actions. Ever since then, I had wondered "why God had misled me." But I realize now that bipolar creates a whole elaborate covey of false relationships and situations—often backed up by some religious goal for me to live out the life of a biblical character... be it Joseph or Paul or Jacob. When in high mania, I have often risen into this kaleidoscope world of time-warps and world-saving.

It's extremely difficult for me, when in the heights of mania, to "have God create me," because one of the main dysfunctions at those times is over-creativity. In the thick of mania, I tend to value my creativity over everything else. It becomes my god, my goal, and my downfall—all at the same time. To let go and "have God create me" is an absolutely counter-intuitive concept to my alter-ego, *Sham*. "God creating me" means to listen to God and to listen to the still, small voice inside. *Sham* won't have it!

*Trust in the Lord with all your heart,*
*and lean not on your own understanding.*

*Proverbs 3:5 (RSV)*

*Sham* has no time to listen because he's too busy creating and relying on his own knowledge for understanding. This creates a mega-self-righteous and self-justifying mentality that forms the basis where denial and unawareness get a foothold. *Sham* uplifts a guise that "everything's all right," even when my world is crashing in on me, and confusion becomes a way of thinking, believing <u>and</u> acting.

I'm beginning to see how God <u>didn't</u> mislead me. In 2008, *Sham*, in his freedom to wander the streets of fantasy and non-reality in my mind, conjured up notions of grandeur and heroism far beyond anything I would have ever dared to dream in my normal state—as *Rich*, the real me. And as *Rich*, I have pretty *realistic* goals and imaginings—not of saving the world from all evil, but of teaching what I have learned—be it bipolar, interpersonal relationships or <u>intra</u>personal relationships (such as self-esteem).

It has been quite disorienting and even frightening to have had thoughts that pointed toward my spirituality as being the culprit in my many manic escapades. I now see that my spirituality was merely a hostage—or worse yet—a slave of the illness' whims. Yet, in all the upheaval of 2008, in all the pain and dismay and nagging insomnia, it was my spiritual life that brought me back to reality.

*It's not what happens to you that makes*
*the difference, it's how you react to it.*

*Dr. Alan Zimmerman*

A breakthrough occurred in late August 2008, as I walked across a Target parking lot near home. I happened to nearly step on one of those dangly things that hangs from the rear view mirror of a car. It was a colorful depiction of "Our Lady of Guadalupe" (Jesus' mother as she is said to have mysteriously appeared in Mexico around 1500 AD). It had been imprinted on a 2 X 3 inch piece of cardboard and was just lying there, being run over by cars. So I gently picked it up and brought it home. This became, in my manic mind, my "sighting of Mother Mary," and I began praying *the Rosary* that day.

What's *the Rosary?* It is a devotional prayer device, featuring 59 beads in a circle, attached to a Crucifix (a cross bearing a replication of the crucified Christ). Praying it (with its 50 "Hail Marys" and 5 "Our Fathers") helped me focus on the life of Jesus—especially in the midst of my lost-ness in Michigan—in September and early October of 2008. *The Rosary* connected me with my faith life like never before, and I truly believe it was the Presence of Mother Mary, in those dark and lonely times, that showed me the way back to the life I was supposed to be living—and am now living.

*The Rosary*, a 20-minute devotion which I have prayed nearly every day since late August, (when I found the Lady of Guadalupe card), has been the structure, the grounding-point, THE WAY for Jesus to find me, and for me to find Him—through the guidance and love of His mother.

How could a regular guy like me start believing in the power of something so mystical, so mysterious as *the Rosary*? Simple. It felt right. It felt right to be imagining the sufferings of Jesus as I prayed the *Sorrowful Mysteries*—and as I envisioned my own sufferings, as they would pop into my mind. It felt right to bubble with joy at the *Joyful Mysteries* of Christ's birth, and his being found safe in the temple. It felt right to experience the exhilaration of Jesus' Resurrection while praying the *Glorious Mysteries*, as my own life lay like dead wood on the side of the road. I *found myself* in *the Rosary*...reflecting a spirituality that I, as a Catholic, could relate to.

*religion*

*expected*

*unchosen*

*makes*

*false faith*

*protected*

*frozen*

*stiff*

*dead*

*but religion uncovered*

*and believed can*

*lead to life*

*and a joy unyielding*

I truly believe that imagination is one of our most precious gifts. Mine has sled me astray many-a-time by *Sham's* influence—hijacked by delusion and misguided thinking. But THIS WAS REAL! The connection, consolation and creativity (healthy and balanced) that has come from praying the Rosary has led me back to safety, (saving this blind man jaunting toward the cliff of despair), and has become a consoling, creative connection between Mother Mary and myself—one which I will always be grateful for and cherish!

So, "LET GOD CREATE ME" is my new spiritual mantra—a fabulous way for me to see my spirituality as benefactor, as friend, as guide—not some dead end road of destructive imagination that I thought it had become. I believe in God much more fully than before 2008's antics began—and I thank God for the 59 beads attached to a Crucifix—*the Rosary*—that lead me home!

*For "everyone who calls upon the name of the Lord will be saved."*

*Romans 10:13 (RSV)*

Yet, as my life has been coming back to orderliness and reality, I have had to let go of many of the symbols of Our Lady of Guadalupe that I had had all around me—around my neck, in my bedroom, in my office. They reminded me too much of my flight to Michigan and the many trials I had put Sandra through. It was freeing to cut the little laminated picture of Our Lady off of my necklace and replace it with a silver and gold cross.

This is a more fitting and enduring symbol of my devotion to Jesus Christ. It's all about being true to myself, and knowing where my real loyalties lie—to my Savior first, and to the Trinity. I truly respect and revere all that Mother Mary did to rear, love and help Her son Jesus become the man He needed to become, yet my loyalties are to Jesus, the Son of God.

Yet, as mentioned before, I believe the influence of Mother Mary was a key factor in bringing me back to my life here in Milwaukee. So *spirituality* wasn't my enemy after all—it was, and is, the saving grace that brings the most meaning and richness to my life, through my relationships and my prayer life. I thank God for these experiences, and for bringing me through them . . . but I pray a relapse like that of 2008 never happens again!!

# *a force of blinding darkness*

*who would believe that many of my deepest*
*spiritual experiences would come my way*
*in the dreary darkness and blinding brightness*
*of this paradoxical traveling companion, bipolar disorder?*

*how could these painfully blind depressive bouts*
*& the blinding elation of manic times be God-filled?*
*it's all in what one considers spiritual*

*I see the "spiritual" as . . .*
*~whatever helps bring us closer to GOD*
*~whatever helps us understand ourselves better*
*~whatever brings us into deeper awarenesses of how*
*to love others and ourselves &*
*~whatever motivates us to give others the blessings given to us*

*THIS is the process my illness has presented me—*
*events not just handed to me*
*but soaking me in the cool rain of blessed possibilities that God*
*has helped transform within me into life-changing lessons~*
*this dark brilliance brings meaning to my existence*
*and grace-filled gifts into my heart and hands*
*ready for me to give to the world*

*would this not be considered an ally?*

# Chapter 6

## the power of red

*To the extent to which we avoid and deny*
*and disown our own experiences,*
*it's clear that we impoverish and diminish our sense of self.*

*Dr. Nathaniel Brandon*

It's a trick to replace the red face of anger with the red heart of love—especially when anger is the driving force of self-righteous indignation swarming around the bee hive of bipolar mania. The anger started after my medication maladjustment in mid-September 2007—my moods rising into a confusing state of what's called "mixed states."

As I understand it, a mixed state is where the mania and depression seem to combine—like when, as a kid, you may have dispensed a packet of Kool Aid powder into a glass pitcher of cold water . . . granules filtering through the water until soon the whole pitcher was bright red. My psychiatrist switched my mood stabilizer for another one, which turned out to be the wrong move for me because it created a mixed state where depression became hidden. This eventually led to a total loss of emotion...not numb—with numbness you at least "feel" like you don't feel anything. With this mixed state, there was just a nothingness, an undetectable emptiness...no hunger or sleepiness, no anger or joy, no ambition or despondency—nothing!

Soon after our wedding (in early October 2007), the mixed state was detected and I was immediately taken off the new mood stabilizer. That's when the anger started to rise. I first began feeling angry at work—which I only expressed away from work. Then, family members became the target—and finally Sandra got the brunt of my flip-flopping emotions. By February 2008, *Sham* had begun to "show up" as I began to go back and forth from "Mr. Nice Guy" to "Mr. Jerk." As I look back, I, *Rich*, was there only part of the time, and my hours of Presence were getting shorter and shorter. Anger became *Sham's* tool of choice for dealing with anything or anyone who got in his way.

On February 14th, a florist bungled a delivery job. *Sham* appeared and took all attention away from the purpose of Valentine's Day—to show love. It was as if the manic energies were being directly transmuted into angry responses. *Sham's* self-righteous "logic" made Sandra's every statement wrong, and every accusation of *Sham's* right. As I look back, I can remember numerous times when I was me, *Rich*, one moment (calm, assertive, amiable), then became *Sham* the next (angry, defiant, back-stabbing)—becoming livid over any small offense by Sandra. It's painful now to see how I came across then.

*Sham* even exclaimed, "Melchers don't do anger!"—a claim that went back many years. He proclaimed that, in my family of origin, it wasn't proper to show a temper or "lose your cool." So, it was simply stuffed, and came out in a passive-aggressive manner. The truth was that this was occasionally MY way of reacting, but not necessarily my family's way. Even when not ill, I didn't handle anger very well, as witnessed below in a poem I wrote about being a teacher's aide in Milwaukee in 1984.

## *Act Yo' Rage*

*(and I'm scared!)*
*scared of the LION inside me*
*"King-of-the-Jungling" all over*
*actin' as if he owns the place*

*he's just like any other animal . . . mortal!*

*and my status takes away my tolerance and my compassion*
*I fall into the trap of supremacy—like back in slave days!*
*me, acting-out with majesty—and red-faced anger!*
*the violence within me starts to screeeeeeeeam*
*to drop peaceful convictions*
*to transform "from Dr. Jekyll into Mr. Hyde"*
*an image I abhor-------and run from!*

*it's me! it's me!!*

*I run from my own ugliness, in shame,...my own evil*
*my own humanness~~no excuses!*
*no reason to act as I do*

*it's when I no longer see the child—only flaming anger and hatred—*
*that I fly off . . . acting the same as my obviously immature students*

*(the worst part is) the child in me submerges like a frightened turtle*
*and the "me" disappears in raging tension*

*(I regret it now)*

This poem, written way back in 1984 (only 4 years after my bipolar diagnosis) shows the beginning stages of *Sham*—although the name and concept of *Sham* only emerged in recent months. Amazing how poetry can capture a mood, or even a personality, in the midst of its adolescence!

Manic anger can be pumped up by the after-burner of "magnification." A common symptom of mania, magnification (the tendency to blow things out of proportion) can cause severe interpersonal destruction. Magnification is evident in this 1985 poem, when life pressures were bearing down on me. This explosive anger is what led to my first hospitalization in early 1986.

un unsu
un sur e

u s ure
n

unsure

fear dances
sorrow smiling

inferiorincapableunstablebrokeninhibited

in the darkness

blackout

shadow walk
gray areas

angerrrrrrrrrrrrrrrrrrrrrrrrrrrrrrrrrrrrrrrrrrrrrrrrrrr bottled
up

hidden

accumulating

can't cry emotional padlock tumblers rusted

truth of worth evades like trying
to catch a feather, grasping in vain, clutching air

self doubt
doubt
d o u b t
d o u b t
d o u b t
d o u b t

Unlike the questioning voice in this 1985 poem, the *Sham* of 2008 was **sure** he was **RIGHT**...he had no doubts. Being right was all that mattered…not someone else's feelings (especially Sandra's), nor anyone else's viewpoint. Sham held his unquestioning stance, even with reality shouting in his face! No stoppin' him! Like a run-away train.

So, what can be learned from all of this? First, bipolar mania will rarely show its face to the person experiencing it. It will hide itself, like a snake in the grass, until one overcomes the denial of reality and the dismissal of others' observations. This transition can be quick, or slow, but must occur for sanity to reappear.

Second, anger must be managed, not ignored. If I were to have been able to recognize the red flags of anger arising at the beginning of 2008, I may have been able to deal with it properly. But, again, the manic cloak kept me from seeing my angry responses, which only escalated with time. Luckily, *Sham* never got physically abusive, although the emotional abuse was quite overpowering.

This quote by Doris Mortman is very significant:

*Until you make peace with who you are,*
*you'll never be content with what you have.*

I discovered that if we have inner conflict, we can't help but create outer conflict. Peace is an inward game, and I have found that a person in severe mania will have great difficulty finding it.

Finally, the bright red hue of a loving heart can be squashed by red-faced anger in a second. Although this anger was pushed in Sandra's face often, she never totally lost hope. She asked me to leave after my final outburst in mid-September, and I stormed out the door—off to my "dream land," Michigan. However, Sandra continued to have faith that I still loved her. Many weeks later, when I called that first day from the hospital in Michigan, she didn't reject me but accepted the fact that I was at least trying to get help. And she has exhibited her love for me more each day, eventually loving me "back into being." And I love her for that—and so much more!

Since I started journaling and writing poetry in 1982—the act of writing had been my biggest blessing. That was until I met and fell in love with Sandra. I know now that SHE has been my greatest gift from God, and I try to express that to her every day—especially now that *Sham* is gone and *Rich* is back!

# *Chapter 7*

## *total projection*

*Ultimately, everything experienced is screened through the filter of our own self-view.*

*Marsha Sinetar*

For Sandra and me, 2008 started with much hope and anticipation... new projects, doors opening, gratitude for gifts given by God. Yet it turned out to be a shaky year for both of us—including an on-again/off-again manic episode for me. I once thought 1986 was the worst year of my life—manic then depressed, then manic again—6 hospitalizations in 12 months. Now I realize that '08 rides on its tail gate, although life has been on the rise since reuniting with Sandra last October.

The successful transition came through my admitting that I had possible bipolar troubles, cooperating with the (Grand Rapids, Michigan) hospital staff, and applying all I've learned about bipolar to my endeavors. Fortunately, after reorienting myself with my various communities back in Milwaukee, I have found a whole new way of life! And the rebuilding of my relationship with Sandra, her family, and my family of origin has been nothing short of miraculous! My relationship with Sandra has never been better!

A friend of mine, Dr. Alan Zimmerman, once proposed that "a crisis will make you either better or bitter...which do you choose?"

Sandra has chosen the way of forgiveness, hope and understanding. She has now become acquainted with *Sham's* influence, and she realizes that *Sham* is a person/personality that does NOT ever have to appear again—as long as I (we) are vigilant in my recovery.

Sandra has become very interested in bipolar, partly because she wants to understand me and help me avoid relapse. Yet, she realizes that the events of 2008 were so devastating for her that she needs to *protect herself* from any further harm, and has chosen to educate herself about bipolar to fend off any further catastrophes. Sandra has embarked on a 12-week course created specifically for loved ones of those who have mental illness, and has bought literature and viewed on-line materials on the topic.

It's sort of like "God did with Job." Job was a man in the Bible who had nearly everything taken away, yet persevered and was given it all back—and then some! This is how I feel…and I have NEVER been more grateful in my life!

Yet, as a part of my re-entry process, (the transformation from *Sham* back to *Rich*) I have come across a striking and mortifying realization that the entire year of 2008 had been lived out in what is called *projection*. This psychological state occurs when one projects one's feelings and impressions—usually a slanted reality—onto others. In my case it was the dastardly trio I groused about all year . . . anger, assumption and self-righteousness.

I was so angry that "Melchers don't DO anger" that I never noticed how upset I was becoming. My *anger* spilled over often as I tried to prove that my family didn't know how to handle their anger. This was like looking in a curved fun-house mirror, and the more my family chose to avoid my impulsive, controlling claims, the angrier I got. It took many weeks after coming back from Michigan to Milwaukee before I had any clue that I had been acting ridiculously. Earlier in 2008, Sandra actually took the brunt of my anger and disappointment. She tried to help me see that my family members were NOT my enemies... but *Sham* had decided otherwise.

*Assumption* was the second part of my finger-pointing act. Being controlled by my alter-ego, *Sham*, I had claimed that my family was "going down" because of all the assuming I thought I saw going on. I felt that their "concerns" about me were really behind–the-back mutterings of what I should be doing to take care of myself. I felt threatened. Yet, influenced by *Sham*, I had been making all the assumptions about the family having so many assumptions. Hmmm…dog chasing its own tail?

The other odd thing was that I had only visited my family once—in early 2008—and was making all these conjectures through intermittent phone calls and e-mails. *Sham* was running on old memories of disappointments, and all the assumptions about the past seemed more important than reality. *Sham* can be devious and pull things from the past, making them seem as though they are happening today.

Then, not to be outdone was *self-righteousness* . . . it was this very quality that *Sham* used exquisitely against me (and everyone around me), stalling any opportunity for me to wake up and "come to my senses." *Sham* had claimed that my family members were being self-righteous in "prescribing" what I should do with my life. Yet, *Sham* was the one who not only had to be right, but WAS right! This kept *Sham* isolated in his "rightness"—physically, intellectually, emotionally, spiritually.

Because of these three projections, *Sham* made it impossible for me to see that people were just trying to do their best...not to mention the fact that no one's perfect AND that no one was out to get me. My expectations were the real problem. No one could meet them because they were unrealistic—and unfair.

Now that I think about it, part of the problem was also jealousy. I have such a highly-gifted family of origin—and my wife and step-family are also very gifted—so much so that I believe I felt intimidated. My own ineptitude to keep a job for more than 5-7 months weighed heavy on my mind and I had difficulty expressing my talents in creative and legitimate ways. I felt disadvantaged, incompetent and incredibly lost—prime territory for *Sham* to dig a foxhole.

I believe it is the "process of admitting"—this radical honesty-enhancing catharsis—that has brought the most change, and the most peace. When I discuss the goings-on of the past year with Sandra, or tap this computer into submission with words of truth and conviction about my recent past, it's as if a hundreds of pounds were lifted from my shoulders.

The realization about how I had been projecting my feelings onto others was a huge breakthrough. And with the inspirations of God through quiet reflection, I was gifted with a modicum of wisdom that no doctor or psychologist had figured out for me. Realizing this has been very affirming!

Ironically, it has been through my greatest screw-ups, my deepest illness and my most notorious moments of unawareness that I have discovered the pearls of compassion, self-validation, hopefulness and self-love . . . not to mention a newly unburied unconditional love for others I never knew I had before.

It all seems to come down to one word—*humility*. I have been given the gift of a peaceful and abiding humility that I never thought possible before. When I begin to judge others or irritability slips in, they are warded off with the sword of strong but gentle humility. It's a whole new world, and I'm grateful I've been given a second chance to experience it!

## *humble*

*in the distance was heard a cry*
*for the meek and mighty to become one*
*it rumbled softly across waving flower beds*
*and gladly rippled upon the silent streams*

*it was a simple calling*
*that brought many to their knees*

*"be kind, be gentle, and love with all humility"*

*and all who listened were brought the graces of the ages*
*for they now knew the longing of God*

# Chapter 8

## *teach what we need most*

A latent seed has germinated in my heart this past week . . . the desire to teach people how to gain self-knowledge and to love themselves better. It arises from recalling a college class I took in 1983, taught by Dr. Alan Zimmerman at Minnesota State University, Mankato. This class, called Interpersonal Communications, was the most important and influential class I've ever taken! In it, Dr. Zimmerman spoke of *self-esteem*—a term that came alive to me just the year before.

I remember it well—it was April 3, 1982—the night I accepted George Benson's "*The Greatest Love of All*" as my theme song, signifying my raison d'être, my purpose.

I just happened to be listening to Benson's 1975 "Weekend in LA" album, and suddenly, I HEARD these life-changing words . . .

*I decided, long ago, never to walk*
*in anyone's shadow*
*If I fail, if I succeed, at least I'll live as I believe . . .*
*no matter what they take from me,*
*they can't take away my dignity!*
*Because the greatest love of all was happening to me . . .*
*I found the greatest love of all inside of me!*

*The greatest love of all is easy to achieve . . .*
*learning to love yourself is the greatest love of all!*

It was as if time stood still, and the words and melody sunk in as deep as the ocean. I grabbed the nicest paper I could find and wrote down the lyrics—the words to a tune which would change my life forever. This song became an omnipresent positive force that has brought me through some extremely tough times.

I've heard it said that "we always want to teach what we most need to learn"...and this is one case that has proved positive in my life—the need to teach about self-esteem and how to promote it in others. Currently, I am creating a speech on self-esteem to present to youth and adult audiences here in Milwaukee. I believe it is extremely important for everyone to see themselves as valuable and competent—to know their goodness and be able to share with others what I call their "*Authentic Greatness*"...the riches of their unique talents and positive personality traits.

Looking deeper, a sense of feeling appreciated is what I'd been lacking the entire year of 2008—if not for my whole life. We all need to be appreciated—an essential component of self-esteem—but my need was so out of proportion that I was never satisfied.

Being newly married to a woman with a totally different style of living and communicating, there were bound to be some unmet expectations and unnerving situations. I had my way of doing things, and Sandra hers, and we both can be pretty stubborn. With my need for approbation so high, I was often left disappointed.

My manic over-humorousness, my over-creativity and my huge need for affirmation were taking a toll on her. The more I was "over the top," the more she shut down...which accelerated my need for a pat on the back, and I tried harder to get it . . . and round, and round it went. It became a vicious cycle that, by August, had come to a head. The anger began to flow. I was irritable, unsatisfied, and *Sham* was showing up more and more. *Sham***,** this deceitful, cunning alter-ego, loved the fact that my self-esteem was low. But something in *Rich* (the real me) kept coming up to the surface. My spirit would not be overrun.

*true self*

*individuality*
*is not a choice*

*it's a fact*
*in order to be*
*A PART OF*
*you need to be*
*a part from*

*the imitator always ends up less*
*because the true self is hidden*
*and*
***only in living the true self***
***can one be free***

*self-knowledge & self-discovery*
*seem the only ways to find this true self -*
*for integrity & wisdom (inner strengths)*
*will shine bright in the person*
*who has found the self*

Seems to me that being whole—body, mind & spirit—IS the goal of having high self-esteem. This *Greatest Love of All* can seem to be sort of a selfish thing, but it actually makes a lot of sense. I don't think it is a brush off of God either. Think about it…if you don't accept yourself, how could you ever accept God's love, the God-Given Graces that come our way so often? Also, how could you love your family and friends if you don't love yourself?

The night I first fell into depression, in January 1980, I had begun questioning whether I could *love others* . . . a clear sign to me now that I was struggling to love myself, to see my own competency and to recognize my gifts and abilities. In fact, I believe the difficulties with bipolar illness "showed up" *because* I was having these self-esteem problems. But, since the illness was going to show its face sometime anyway, maybe it was best that it did so my senior year of high school instead of at college when I was away from home and under higher scholastic pressure.

No wonder I want to teach youth about the treasures of high self-esteem and the pitfalls of its opposite. I don't want anyone else to go through the struggles I went through. But I have been hard on others' self-esteem also. I once wrote, "Comes a time when we see that in hurting another we really hurt ourselves—and the toll can be high!"... case in point, my encounter with Raymond.

It was my first year in Milwaukee, fall of 1984, when my housemate, Denny, needed a fill-in for his $6^{th}$ grade catechism class at the parish where he was a youth pastor. The problem was that I had very poor boundaries and, at times, had a level of immaturity comparable to that of a $6^{th}$ grade student—or, as you will see, probably less advanced.

I had arrived early for the 9:30 a.m. class, and at 9:25, my first student sauntered over the threshold—Raymond. He sat near the front of the class, unusual for an 11-year-old boy. I was busy readying my talk at the front of the room and didn't notice, at first, the snapping noise. Raymond was showing another student how to SNAP the erasers off my pencils which I had brought for an exercise in my program.

When I realized the "malaise" (in MY mind), I reacted aggressively with "Who do you think you are?! Those aren't your pencils! I brought those for an exercise later…how are we supposed to use them now?! You've ruined them!!"

Startled, Raymond grabbed his jacket and headed for the door. Before disappearing, he leaned his head back in and gruffly retorted, "YOU'RE A TERRIBLE TEACHER!!"

My ire riled and my self-righteous denial kept me from seeing that, indeed, he was right…at that moment, I WAS a terrible teacher! I had trashed him for such a silly offense.

*The nature of an individual's self-evaluation has profound effects on the individual's thinking processes, emotions, desires, values and goals.*

*Dr. Nathaniel Brandon*

So what if he had "popped" a few pencils—deed done—my over-reaction was un-called-for. But what **was** I doing to this young man's sense of self? Looking back, I believe the reason I was so upset was that the kids at the grade school where I was a teaching had been *popping my pencils* too, and I had had it! Raymond was my payback, unconsciously. I had no idea I was doing anything wrong…lost in unawareness and insensitivity. Shame, humiliation, unleashed anger—Raymond got it all. And you won't believe what my talk was about that morning . . . yes…self-esteem! Irony of ironies!

*Within every problem you face, there is the potential for growth, and regardless of what the answer is, you should always be alert to the growth which the problem is inviting you to undergo.*

*J. Douglas Bottorff*

It has been through humbling experiences such as this that God has built compassion, understanding and hope within me. Yet, looking at 2008, what is self-esteem to a man divided?...a man who abandoned his wife and his life, and whose illness had nearly ruined his life? How can lessons-learned actually be applied to bipolar imbalance?

It means keeping my self-esteem high so that *Sham* never dares to, or has the chance to, come out again! When I know myself and feel good about myself—and when I can express myself appropriately—*Sham* will not have the negative emotions and the "evidence" to stage a mutiny again. The scary thing is that my encounter with Raymond in 1984 was an early version of 2008's *Sham*—a precursor, of sorts. If only I had been aware of it then...unawareness can be devastating!

Self-esteem and mental health are certainly linked. The medication adjustment I had at the Grand Rapids hospital in early October of 2008 has had a lot to do with my recovery process. Without my brain chemistry shift (brought on by the appropriate medications) and the ensuing "normal" thought patterns, no self-esteem-promoting attempts would have been effective. So I give a lot of credit to my doctors and staff, over the years, for their wisdom and foresight in helping me reach this balance. Having bipolar balance is such a great thing—offering feelings of security, well-being and joy!

## *under their care*

*in a setting overwhelming*
*when I wasn't seeing straight, much less aware*
*I've found myself in the hands of pros*
*who kept me safe—under their care*
*and when the waves of life crashed in*
*with pain I could not bear*
*they calmed my heart and soothed my fears*
*and soon I walked free—under their care*

*how grateful I am that in the worst of moments*
*I had compassion and skills everywhere*
*cuz at the time I could not make it on my own and*
*recovery staff held me—under their care*

# *Chapter 9*

## *the gift of tears*

*"…look, my eyes are dry,*
*the gift was ours to borrow…"*

*Broadway play, A Chorus Line*

It's strange how the most harrowing times of our lives can also be the most grace-filled. When I drove off to Michigan in late August 2008—the most up-and-down year of my life—I brought along with me a precious gift…tears.

By that time, *Sham* was ruling the roost 100% of the time and I, *Rich* (the healthy me) had been bound and gagged and crammed behind the captain's seat—a man gone missing. Some call it being "out of your mind." I can see that. *Rich* was out—out of his mind and *Sham* was IN it. Does that mean I was insane? Hmmmm…"insane"… pretty harsh word. But, strange as it may seem, now looking at it from the viewpoint of sanity, this could very well be the correct language. The interesting and touching aspect of this is that *Sham* never cried a tear—*Rich* did. I, *Rich,* cried nearly 30 times in a two month period...most times with "gushing" tears, sometimes with just a moist eye, but always with a sincere heart.

They say tears are "cleansing." I add that they are "connecting." Although *Sham* controlled my consciousness for the 7 weeks I was in Michigan, two things kept *Sham* from total dominance: "*Rich's* tears" and a consistent devotion to Mother Mary through *the Rosary*. Yes, praying *the Rosary* (with its 59 beads and a crucifix) had become a priority in August, but why were tears important? Why talk about them at all?

I mention tears because they played such a huge role in saving me from impending doom and a life of disconnection from all that I love. It was in those tearful moments that I was most sincere, most real, most ME. I cried for specific reasons each time—either over loneliness, feelings of loss, or in prayer for loved ones...and, in doing so, kept the connection between *Rich* and my loved ones on-going. Without the tears & the free-flowing goodness of their regenerating purpose, I believe *Rich* would have been lost for a much longer time, and the relationships may never have been recovered.

I've cried only once since returning to Milwaukee in October 2008. These lone tears happened at Christmas while I was watching (for the 20th time) "*It's a Wonderful Life*," the Christmas movie with Jimmy Stewart. It always chokes me up when Stewart, as George Bailey (the movie's main character) runs to the snowy bridge, begging for his guardian angel, Clarence, to give him his life back. Rarely do you see a man cry in the movies (or in "real" life), but there was George, sobbing, repeating over and over, "I wanna live again! I wanna live again!" Deep inside, I believe this was *Rich's* unspoken plea, too, in all the wanderings in Michigan.

This scene is so REAL to me! It is one of what I call my *"Troubadours"...those events, people & things that bring life to Life...that make us who we are, and inspire us to become our best selves!* This scene has played over and over in my mind and heart for many years. And tears often accompany the emotional tug I get when I see it.

I believe in God-Given Graces ("G³s") and I KNOW my tears in August, September and early October of 2008 were Heaven-sent. "I cried a river," as the song goes, and none of it was wasted water. And I thank God for this saving grace, but I know I may never cry like that again…*the gift was mine to borrow.* Hopefully, I won't have THAT much to cry about in the future!

# *Chapter 10*

## *"diss-abled"*

*"...the way I see it, you can either run from your past or learn from it..."*

*(wise baboon in Lion King)*

Speaking with my oldest brother John the other day, I told him of my many job applications and the disappointing outcomes of three job interviews. In this job market, it's extremely difficult for one to find a position that matches one's skills and abilities.

John pointed out to me, very gently, that because of the employment struggles caused by my illness, I would probably qualify for Social Security Disability (which I will call "Disability"). He said this could be "a Holy Spirit thing," in that I would be able to volunteer at schools, hospitals and treatment centers that may not be able to afford a consultant because of budgetary constraints.

This struck a chord in me—that I could be helped along financially with Disability AND do the writing, speaking and teaching I've wanted to do for years. So, I decided to take an inventory of my employment history, and found that I have left 70% of my previous jobs because of bipolar-related circumstances! I was shocked! I had no idea my illness had been so detrimental to my work history!

I had received Disability back in 1992 for 12 months or so, yet felt quite uncomfortable receiving it. I had been working part-time as a custodian, but I didn't want to tell others that I was receiving Disability. I didn't want to be stigmatized—to be seen as *less-than* because I have a mental illness.

The youth have a term for showing lack of respect called "dissing"—which means DISSrespecting. I've dealt with the possibility of being considered "diss-abled," and, for fear of being "dissed" by others, I have often kept my bipolar a secret, especially in the work environment. But, now that I think about it, in 2003, I spoke directly to youth twice about my experiences with bipolar at the school with which I was a teacher's aide in Minnesota. I wasn't *dissed* during or after by the students, yet I think the teachers present felt quite uncomfortable with it.

A similar uneasiness revealed itself in my Toastmasters public speaking group around the same time. I gave a speech on bipolar that lasted 10 minutes, and the speech evaluator gave me a six minute evaluation—twice as long as the time allotted! That wouldn't have been a big deal other than that she gave me six minutes of negative comments! Baffled by why this evaluator was so out of character in length and tone, I asked another member what she thought had happened. I was told that the evaluator had told her she was thrown so off guard and felt so uncomfortable with my speech content, that she completely lost the ability to give a balanced evaluation.

I guess it goes both ways because I feel uncomfortable when the question arises in social situations..."What do you do for a living?" Sandra and my mom both answered that question in unison recently by proclaiming, "*You're a writer!*" No need to go further, they concluded. But it's not that easy, especially when others may say "Who do you write for?" It could make for some pretty uncomfortable encounters. Fact is, writing & speaking is my occupation! It is what I am *occupied* with—often for more than four hours a day, seven days a week.

I guess a part of receiving Disability would mean a shift in perspective, and possibly a welcomed one...a feeling that, once again, I would be able to offer financial assets in my relationship with Sandra.

But getting disability may also be like getting "a shot in the arm" and a punch in the face at the same time. It's energizing to think about grasping the opportunities for speaking and teaching, but it's de-energizing to think about the fact that I would not be "earning" any money . . . a mixed bag, but not a hopeless one.

I love what Darlene Larson Jenks once wrote:

*To do nothing is failure.*
*To try, and in the trying make some mistakes,*
*and then to make some positive changes*
*as a result of those mistakes,*
*is to learn & grow & blossom.*

It's been a life of crashing down and scraping myself up off the pavement again. With 18 hospitalizations and many broken-hearted situations, maybe it's just a matter of coming to my senses that brings me to this point. And will I even qualify for Disability? I have no idea. But I really don't want to get into an overly-stressful job situation again, and have stress bring *Sham* creepy-crawling out of his cave to attempt to destroy my life in his blind disruptiveness. Maybe Disability is a next step in making peace. At this point, God only knows.

## *tested by fire*

*Lord, oh Lord, raise me higher*
*may I not be tested by fire*
*tested by water—You keep me from drowning*
*tested by wind—the trees sway surrounding*

*but give me the grace*
*to live well in this place*
*& may I not be tested by fire*

*when my vision's a blur*

*and my mind confused*
*You see me and act before*
*all my patience is used*

*when I'm suffering too much*
*You drive evil away*
*You bless me by night*
*and protect me by day*

*You give me a way*
*to see Your truth again*
*I give You my heart*
*and I gain a best friend*

*Lord, please give me the grace*
*to live well in this place*
*and may I not be tested by fire!*

# *Chapter 11*

## *Zest*

*If we meet our challenges with a zest for adventure,*
*we will gain even from our losses.*

*Dynamics of Personal Motivation*

This has been one of the most challenging quotes I have ever encountered because it strikes to the core of my condition—whether it be bipolar, melancholy, lack of motivation or just LIFE. Often I don't know why I experience the emotional states that I do. Many days, I'll be feelin' fine, then my day can quickly spin into an ugly little piece of depression. But one important thing I've recently come to know is that, in any downward spin, I can be assured that "*this is a tendency, not a disposition*"...that this mood (which is not produced by a chemical imbalance) is not ME...it is not my basic character, but a way of thinking and feeling that can be modified with a little insight and effort.

Some factors that have led to a sub-par state of emotional wellness are unemployment, stalling job opportunities, a basement in disarray, (a state caused by moving all my stuff out in September of '08 and back into the basement in November), and a lack of purpose.

Much of it has to do with the unemployment aspect. I feel in limbo, having registered for Disability and hoping for an interview with an urban prep school simultaneously. Also, I've had three job interviews in the past two months, with two sending me a letter stating "you're not the one," and the other never calling me back. Plus I've applied for five other jobs and not heard a thing. Rejection gets old after a while.

But how can I have *a zest for adventure* right now? How can I *gain even from my losses?* **Attitude**. It's an attitude thing…and the attitude I choose is K.O.K.O…."Keep On Keepin' On!" Now is the time to step up and plant my feet in the reality of GIFTS GIVEN…gifts given to me to enjoy, and gifts given to me to share with others.

*You'll never change your life if*
*you wait 'til you feel like it!*

*Dr. Alan Zimmerman*

It is in these times of desolation that I need to seek consolation by doing just what I've been doing…spending quality time with Sandra, writing this book, reading my spiritual readings, praying my *Rosary* and working on my speeches. *This is my job right now*! I work in the home ½-time, and improving my communication skills is my job. I don't "laze around"—actually I'm quite busy!

It was this attitude of K.O.K.O. that, without having a name for it at the time, kept me going in all the depressive moments in my past… although often I had probably just waded through the muck, trying to get by. Yet, when not chemically imbalanced, wouldn't it just take a wave of my hand to change my attitude from one of lack to one of abundance?

Well,…yes! Since I believe I do not have a chemically-imbalanced type of "depression" occurring, it IS merely a change of attitude, a shift of behavior that can make all the difference.

*I could choose to see this situation*
*as a setback or a starting point.*

*W Mitchell*

The inspiration for writing this chapter—prompting a change of attitude—was a walk in the freezing January Wisconsin air...3 p.m., sunny, breezy and very cold. It was this change of atmosphere that helped me start to bust out of the ice-block-consciousness I found myself experiencing—a day with NOTHING in my planner but a quick repair for Sandra's car. When I have "nothing to do," there always seems to be trouble lurking.

I know, from my understanding of REBT (Rational Emotive Behavioral Therapy) that our *thoughts create our feelings*, not the other way around. My atmosphere, my empty calendar, my lack of employment...they are <u>not</u> creating how I feel about myself—<u>my thoughts</u> about them are! If my calendar is empty, I need to fill it with anything that can keep me constructively busy (such as cleaning up that basement!) Come on, Rich!

If I'm feeling bad about the possibility that the prep school job opportunity may not have come through, I need to look forward and onward to the next good possibility by checking the internet for potential jobs. I'm not option-less, and NOT as helpless as I seem to believe I am, at times.

I like what my dad's late business partner, Wayne, once told me: "<u>There's ALWAYS something to do!</u>" I remember his enthusiasm about getting me to read a National Geographic article on Africa, and how he invited me, at age 11, to go on a fishing trip to Northern Minnesota with my brother. I have used his "*always something to do*" proclamation to promote common sense and hard work dozens of times! I'll always remember this simple but profound advice!

One of the ways I pull myself out of a dive is by creating what I call "ST. LOFT": *<u>S</u>omething <u>T</u>o <u>LO</u>ok <u>F</u>orward <u>T</u>o*. When life is dragging me down a bit, I've been found writing at least three activities in my day planner the night before so I had *something to look forward to*. I haven't been doing this lately, but now, I will again. This urges me on to be productive, especially when I'm struggling to keep this virtue in view.

ST. LOFT is a helpful reminder...like tonight—Sandra and I are going to Madison, Wisconsin, just over an hour from Milwaukee, to stay in a hotel so she will be perky for chairing a meeting there tomorrow morning…ST. LOFT! And we've got a great movie at home that we're eager to watch...ST. LOFT! And I'm participating in an all-day Christian men's conference this coming weekend...ST. LOFT!

It's so easy to go into a haze of self-pity and negativity, isn't it? When things aren't going as planned, when we have no plans at all, or when passivity and even hopelessness edge their way in the door, we need to choose to meet these challenges...with A ZEST FOR ADVENTURE!!

## *What with one day?*

*What would my day be like if I*
*had but one day to live?...*
*No tomorrow*
*No next week*
*Only today*

*What would I do with it?*
*Would I experience joy over this one last chance*
*to do the simple loving things around me?*
*or experience dread over all I had left behind?*

*Would I see an opportunity opening before me to do*
*one last good deed for my neighbor*
*or close up like a clam in shame and self-pity*
*as though my life had not mattered?*

*Would I write that one last loving letter to a friend,*
*a family member or to the world?*
*Or would I have no letters to share but*

*I. G. I. V. E. U. P. ?*

*Imagine the amazing fact that—when you take a good look—*
*This IS all we've got...*Now IS All There IS
*and we only get one go-around...*

*That day of joy or dread is reality!*
*The opportunities opening or closing are happening!*
*That letter we lovingly write may just be our last!*

*What's keeping you from living this day as if it were your last?*
*And WHAT could you imagine as being a better motivator in your life?*

*Try it for a day—but remember...*
***Today never ends!***

# *Chapter 12*

## *Precious*

Amazing how time can play with our minds. The poem below was created only five days after the July 2008 debacle in Chicago where I trashed the coach training program and lost my dream in the process. Seems like a lifetime ago—AND seems like just yesterday!...actually, it was six months ago.

### *the Fountain of YOU*

*You, God, are the fountain of my soul*
*this water that streams so high and free*
*belongs to You*
*even though most others see it as*
*my gifts, my talents, my expression*

*yet now I know*
*You're not only the fountain*
*but the water itself!*

*and me?*
*simply the form, the height, the force*

*that Your Spirit sends me*
*up & down & through & out & up again*

*what a blessing—what a gift of humility—to see*

*that You are the very* ***essence*** *of my being*
*and as I grasp to realize that I once thought*
*I was that water—or even the fountain . . . ?*

*sometimes humility comes only through the recognition*
*of our reach for significance . . . which then points*
*to our precious indispensability*

At the moment this poem was created, I adopted a whole new and wonderful mind-set about who God is in my life—*the fountain.* In seeing the fountain outside the Chicago hotel where the coach training program was being held, my image of God—and my personal view of bipolar—shifted. I no longer put the pressure on myself that I had to "do it by myself." Seeing the water spurt up & out and into the air helped me see that I was not the center of the world after all—only a fountain-born creation who *contributes* to the purpose of the world. And bipolar was merely part of the form the water was taking. (At least I got <u>something</u> good out of that life coaching weekend!)

My alter-ego, *Sham*, had his own plans for which way my life would head, though—a downhill ride all the way. But, as *Sham* has retreated into the shadowed valley of my subconscious, I now see an upward spiral—my soul reaching to new heights each day. I KNOW God has something wonderful *planned* for me. But since I don't believe in *predestination* (the belief that God's got EVERYTHING planned and we're just here to watch it play out), I see that we all have a personal influence on all that happens to us.

This scene from the movie *Forrest Gump*, reflects this philosophy and has played a significant role in my emotional and spiritual development:

The Spirituality of Forrest Gump
(From the movie Forrest Gump):
" . . . I don't know if Mama was right
or if it's . . . if it's Lieutenant Dan . . .
I don't know if we each have a . . . destiny;
or if we're all just floatin' around
accidental-like, on a breeze . . . but, I think . . .
I think it's BOTH----maybe both happening
at the same time . . ." (Forrest Gump played by
Tom Hanks)

In a nutshell, THIS is a major component of my belief system! I believe that God plays a huge role, but our efforts also play a crucial part. As Forrest Gump implied, it's both grace and chance.

Why is this book called Discerning Bipolar Grace? Because I am in the process of trying to figure out how God's grace is working in my life, as I've struggled with bipolar—and as I *discern* who/what/when/where/why/how I am to act.

I believe that life is a process, not a *procession*. If it were a procession, all we'd have to do is play our little part and move on down the line. But as "process," I see life as being an endless jigsaw puzzle, a winding road and a grand adventure—all at the same time! Irving Berlin said:

*Life is 10% what you make it*
*and 90% how you take it.*

When I first read this quote, I had no clue what it meant. Now I see that, for me, it means that our perception—the way we interpret things—is the biggest factor in how life evolves. Before "The Fountain,"

I saw myself as the focal point of all I do. Then suddenly the focus became God, and I was the *utterance* of God—not the vocal cord or the thought, just the sound itself.

*"...whoever speaks is to do so as one*
*who is speaking the utterances of God..."*

*1 Peter 4:11 (RSV)*

As I reflect on *The Fountain*, I recognized what "form" others have taken—the roles they have played to better my life. I distinctly remember a moment in my life when the "utterance" of an acquaintance in high school altered my course—my deepest inner-workings. When I was seriously depressed during the spring of my senior year in high school, a classmate I barely knew taped a card on my locker, stating that I looked discouraged, and she hoped I'd feel better soon. Sounds like no big deal, right? No big deal?

That card literally saved my life! Not one of my "real" friends had even mentioned that I looked tired or sad! And I don't see myself as THAT great of an actor to have been fooling them for four months. I think they were just caught up in themselves and didn't take time to really notice how dragged-out I looked and sounded. But this one person, this "someone" I didn't know very well, reached out to me and pulled me back from the edge that day. The relief may have only lasted for a day or two, and then I was "back on the ledge" of despair again. But she saved me **that** day.

I've thought about the lesson I learned hundreds of times. In contemplating the card I received that day in 1980, I've come to believe that one of the most important written contributions I've ever made to this world has been gifted to me—thanks to "the card connection." It comes from the heart of my experience and the depth of my soul:

*"We will never ever really know how we will affect others—*
*so we need to always be a good example!"*

It is not in our power to know exactly what is going on in another's heart, mind and soul. We need to realize that a person who seems so upset behind the store counter, the person who cuts us off in traffic, or the co-worker who seems so insolent and distant MAY BE having one of the worst day of their lives—teetering on the edge of despair at that very moment. Have you ever thought that your response to them may make the difference between a potentially positive or a dramatically negative outcome? Your influence may be as simple as a smile or a moment of patience.

How do you know that the gruff bus driver may or may not have lost his wife that day—hence having a more-than-grumpy demeanor? Or that the rude customer service rep on the other side of the phone may have found out the day before that she has cancer? It is our compassion and good will, no matter if we see the distress in the eyes of another or not, that displays our integrity.

This is why "we need to always be a good example," and try to give the other a break. It's not easy to do, and I feel hypocritical for even suggesting it because I don't always do so. But I believe this is our call…THIS is what my Christian faith is all about—to love without knowing how my love will be received. It is what is within our hearts, our true character, our *Authentic Selves* that needs to be the center of our being…not the big job, or the big car or boat, or the prestige underlying it all. Oliver Wendell Holmes had it right when he wrote . . .

*What lies behind us and what lies ahead of us*
*are tiny matters compared to what lies within us.*

This was what touched me so deeply that day in high school—the card that changed my life----saved my life! For some reason God allows us to go through such moments of utter agony, only to be rectified by the observant kindness of another. Do YOU display this type of *observant kindness* in your daily dealings? I hope you do.

There was another person who reached out to me—with dignity and generosity—my senior year of high school . . . my mother. She was there for me—in it with me—laying herself down in front of me to bridge the gap between forlorn lost-ness and an unknown future she envisioned as hopeful. Without my mom, I would certainly not be touching these keys at this moment and would have lost my life that spring for sure.

But she was just being herself. She couldn't help it! She has never acknowledged to me that she thought she was doing anything dramatic or outstanding—but simply being a mother. Still, I have made it clear to her many times how much it meant to me the day she just sat with me as I blankly stared at the living room ceiling in April of 1980. Or how she whipped up some hot chocolate on the mornings I would steal behind the garage until my dad went to work. I would then come lagging up the stairs into the house, avoiding school at any cost.

These "tiny" loving moments are examples of her "Presence"—**just being there** for me. It could be simply holding the hand of a grandmother in a coma, or caressing the head of a weeping child—millions of variations—but all so crucial. This is what makes us human. And what can we give back? Nothing—nothing but gratitude. It doesn't have to be to the person at that time, but, do you think I haven't shown gratitude toward my "card-giver" over the years? Dozens of times...gratitude that turned into loving actions toward others! And she will <u>never</u> know it. She will never know how she affected me (*unless she reads this book*)—or the ripple effect of the love she caused to occur. But thank God she reached out!

My own home-spun word that describes gratitude is "*gratitudinous*"—an adjective I use when I express gratitude for gifts given. It has become one of the top five components of my spiritual life—and may just be #1. Gratitude is the most precious gift we can give—to God, to others and to the world. My acronym "TUG", used often in my journal, is my way of saying "<u>T</u>hank <u>U</u> <u>G</u>od", and is my term of endearment for THE FOUNTAIN who makes my life what it is—a blessing…a life filled with Grace.

Rich Melcher

# Gratitude

sun setting in cool April sky
but for the Grace of God go I
a day gone by and I hadn't thought
or noticed gifts given I had not sought

it hit me hard to serve a meal
to the disadvantaged, the poor—for real
and in their faces I saw myself
my hidden ghost upon a shelf

but when I closed the door to leave
God said to me "Do you not believe
these very people you served today
could have been you, or could be you someday?"

my throat tightened with a throbbing heart
as I realized I'd forgotten the most important part
of my faith, religion and spirituality
it is gratitude that needs to be most important to me

for it is God's Almighty plea
for us to know and come and see
that thankfulness is a grand virtue
as faith and hope and love are too

as I drove away in awe of God's Grace
with a simple message and a smile on my face
"to say 'thanks' as often as I say 'please'
and to see Him in the least of these"

# *Chapter 13*

# *Changes*

*Some of our greatest learnings come through the process of moving from deep disappointment to transformative enlightenment.*

*Rich Melcher*

One can never fully predict what will occur when a group of people gather for a (seemingly) common purpose. Yesterday, it was an all-day Catholic men's conference that filled my planner. I expected maybe 200-300 men of all ages, races and backgrounds; I experienced no teens, or men in their 20s, a few in their 30s and the rest in their 40s, and up—ALL white (including myself). And, backgrounds?...I found out I was among a group of men who seemed to be primarily conservative Catholics. How do I know "conservative"?

Well, "cultish" would be a better take on the atmosphere! It was a self-promoting, exclusive, "old school" event, with its emphasis on how "Catholic is the ONLY way to go" and confession is the only REAL way to be freed from guilt caused by sin.

I felt like a Jew in the middle of a Hitler youth rally when the lecturing priest stated he would <u>never</u> vote for a man who "supported abortion" (referring to Barack Obama)...and the crowd of 3,000 men cheered, clapping their hands loudly in righteous approval. I was stunned, spinning into an eerie self-conscious awareness that I was in a spiritually dangerous atmosphere.

I lasted through lunch, determined to make it through the conference, when the same priest began answering questions that participants had written on cards. I heard him say, "Priests <u>cannot</u> get married because JESUS WAS NOT MARRIED." That didn't go down very well with me. I believe the Catholic Church will be nearly out of priests in 20-30 years if they do not—very soon—allow priests to marry, accept women as priests, or both. That's my opinion, for what it's worth.

But then the priest said that only *practicing* Catholics—who have received First Communion AND who *follow **every** teaching* of the Catholic Church—can receive Holy Communion (Eucharist)! My gears were ground and my circuits were fried…I could stand no more! I left immediately.

This was to be my time to connect with men, my time to be enriched in my Catholic faith, my time to get away and learn something new. The only thing I learned was that there are some sick organizations out there (such as this men's conference) promoting a lot of twisted and warped ways of looking at God and religion…Spirituality was *never even touched* there, in my opinion—what I went there for in the first place.

## *I AM*

*I am who I am*
*what I am*
*where I am*
*because of my struggles*

*SUFFERING*

*but I don't go back and thank those*

*who flung their burdens on me*

*I don't go back and greet those who shut me out*
*and labeled me unacceptable*

*I don't go back and chum with the ones who smashed my*
*free-flowing friendship on the jagged rocks of jealousy and envy*

*I choose only to forgive them and*
*thank God for giving me the wisdom and tolerance*
*to keep travelin' on*

I see the difference between religion and spirituality as night and day. Religion is rules, precepts and "beliefs" set out by a hierarchy to govern the realm of what they see as "God." Religion has its beauty, its order and its connectedness, but it can be a bit limiting.

Spirituality, to me, is the encounter with our Highest Power, in whatever form that may take. It *may be* in a religious setting, or nature, or a support group meeting, or a conversation with a trusted friend… or the solitude of one's own mind and heart.

Don't get me wrong—I am a "religious man," in many ways…I practice the Catholic faith because—well, partly because I was reared that way…yet also because I like it (most of it). I feel uplifted by the Catholic Mass, in so many ways—especially in the Black Catholic tradition in which I worship. But I am a *spiritual* man first and foremost! I believe that my relationship with God is the most important relationship I have, second only to my relationship with myself…then comes Sandra, my mom, and so on. And my relationship with God goes everywhere with me. It is not necessarily contained between the walls and roof of <u>any</u> church. Spirituality—being connected with the Spirit of God—is a crucial focus of my life.

Disappointment seemed to be the order of the day, as I drove off from the men's conference, toward home in the chilly Wisconsin noontime air. Upon reaching home, I found a tremendously empathetic wife who was open to hearing every detail of my difficult morning. My perception of the Catholic Church had been shaken and I was in need of some healing... something to hang onto as the river of false teaching (or, at least what I considered misguided thought and action) pulled on me, threatening to drown me in its swift currents.

Sometimes Grace comes at the most unlikely moment. Sandra had, for weeks, urged me to go with her to get a pedicure. I thought, "Men don't GET pedicures. Anyway, my feet are so nasty—no one would even try to touch them. No way!" Well, after the disillusioning men's conference, I thought, "What the heck. What can I lose but the ends of a few toenails." So off we went.

I continued to talk about the conference, then, just as we rolled into the parking lot of "Magic Nails," I spouted out, "Yeah, the pro baseball player who spoke at the conference about blowin' out his knee has *his* story…and a little kid with leukemia has *his* story, and a woman who survives breast cancer has *her* story…if *I* were to give a hero's speech, what would MY story be? 'I'm crazy!!'" We both giggled as we pulled up to the curb. Suddenly I realized, "Yes—that's it! I have been 'crazy,' and come back from the edge—many times! THIS IS my hero's story! And the fact that it is taboo to speak about—that it may be uncomfortable to tell my story—is exactly why I need to tell it! It is the *stigma* of mental illness that is killing us—and keeping us in the dark!"

During my entire pedicure, my pen chiseled away at my mini notebook, as I scratched out the speech I would give—to youth, to adults, to mental health groups, to anyone and everyone who would listen. My anger from the disappointing morning had subsided and my healing had begun.

*Don't hate the problem—love the solution.*

*Christine Gillette Miller*

I've given over a dozen of speeches on bipolar in my day—to youth and adults—so the prospect of shifting my attention from self-esteem to bipolar was a natural one. Although I have a few self-esteem speeches to be presented soon, I have decided now to concentrate my efforts on speaking to various audiences about bipolar and the general topic of society's overcoming the stigma related to mental illness. I feel much more focused and am rejuvenated by the possibilities this venture may have in store. As my friend Dr. Alan Zimmerman said, "Every problem IS an opportunity," and my time is NOW! I believe this awakening, coming from a day of deep disappointment, was God saying, "Speak from the heart about what you REALLY know about... and do it up right!" And this I intend to do!

A former pastor once had me captivated, with pen in hand, when he said,

> *"The key to life is not in the possessions you accumulate; it is what you become in the growth process of taking your gift and freely giving it away."*

It's as if the "no response" from the prep school I intended to interview with, applying for Disability, and the realization that I could really make a difference in the area of others' understanding of bipolar have merged, and I have a whole new vision of my future. People are probably not going to be able to afford to have a speaker come into their school or organization at $100 per speech...but I can come in as a volunteer and share my insights and experiences...all for the small fee of attention paid, participation afforded and feedback given. This could be my payment to society for the Disability check I would receive...just as my brother John had spoken of weeks ago! This may just be a solution to the cognitive dissonance I have felt these past days in conjunction with whether to seek work or go on Disability. God only knows.

Stephen R. Covey, author of The Seven Habits of Highly Effective People, describes what he calls a "paradigm shift"—a major change in one's overall view of things. This is what happened to me today—a paradigm shift!

Recognizing that I have a strong ambition for sharing my experiences and insights about bipolar changed how I look at the purpose of my life. I sense the dawning of a powerful sense of self, unlike anything I've ever felt. It was so freeing and refreshing to find this gleaming facet of my *Authentic Self*—just resting there, waiting to be rediscovered! I thank God for new awakenings and new opportunities to *learn*! We can learn from the simplest things.

## *icicles*

*icicles*
*drip, drop, drip*
*reaching to touch snow below*
*African drum beat pounds*
*its ancient rhythm*
*echoing across still winter whiteness*
*nature-born*
*melt freeze layer upon layer*

*(life is so)*

*teach me, clear icicles, to take the chance*
*to risk non-existence*
*to broaden my base and lengthen my tolerance*

*you bleed, bleeding the only blood you know*
*pain of the melt brings profit of the freeze*
*feeling the heat and not backing away in fear*
*hanging in there—waiting…waiting*
*(if only I could do as much)*

*alive, as I am—yet only for a short while*

*I admire you, icicles*
*satisfied in teaching me that*
*in comparison*
*I only live as long*

*do I choose to challenge the sun—*
*or rest in the shadows?*

# Chapter 14

## *third nerve*

Have you ever encountered a person who annoys you to no end? Sandra calls it someone "*getting on her third nerve!*" Extreme annoyance! Our relationship has had its *third nerve* qualities—especially in 2008, when I often lost my boundaries, and became extremely defensive—and made a pun of nearly every statement. I couldn't listen when Sandra would tell me, half-jokingly, "Nobody likes a smart aleck!" It just didn't register in my psyche.

Bipolar has a unique quality causing one to ignore the obvious and repeat offensive behaviors over and over. I remember when I went back to Milwaukee for six months, breaking away from Minneapolis where I had returned to in 1986—after my first breakdown. That first night back in Milwaukee, I dropped in on some friends and repeatedly called one young woman "Aretha Franklin" because she had a likeness to the great singer. Problem was, Aretha was quite overweight at the time, and, as I look back, this young lady probably felt the comparison was to her weight, not her facial features (as I had intended). This angered her greatly—I got on her *third nerve.*

Was I trying to be cruel? No. I was, in my manic state, simply unaware—and very inappropriate. I bet most of us have done something similar—been insensitive—but it can be an absolute blindness for those of us in mania. As mentioned earlier in the book, we all most likely encounter a phenomenon called *the Observer. The Observer* is that part of the human mind that simply watches and listens—merely recording the scene. In these cases of my manic inappropriateness, the *Observer's* efforts of documentation have been unencumbered by the ridiculous behaviors, and the situations where others' feelings were hurt.

Why is this significant? Because when someone in mania comes down from the manic state, the remorse and shame of past offenses can be devastating. And *the Observer* is there with every detail readily available.

In 1989, I became enraged and "trashed" my parents' home—not severely—but it was quite messy when I was finished with my tirade. For those antics, I was sent to a state hospital for four months, with plenty of time to consult my *Observer* about my infractions.

It was a very humbling experience—and a confusing one. The shame of what I had done rested heavily on my heart. When my parents came for a conference with my doctor, after I had been there for a month, I desperately wanted to apologize to my dad because most of the destruction was focused on his belongings. My mania had magnified past disappointments and feelings of anger, and it had come down on him.

When I finally apologized to my dad, he said that he wouldn't accept my apology because, as he put it, "It wasn't you." This was distressing. In 1989, I hadn't yet made the *Sham*-distinction, and I insisted it *WAS* I who did those things! After much persuasion, he acquiesced and accepted my apology. The encounter left all of us bewildered. Who WAS this person who threw his father's belongings out the third floor window and smashed his desk chair in the street at 3 a.m.? My *Observer* provided the memories; I provided the negative outlook.

These events had gone so far beyond annoyance, into deep hurt and disillusionment. What were they going to do with a son who could potentially become physically violent with them the next time? Thankfully, that was the only time in my life that I've displayed this explosive anger.

But what has been <u>my</u> manic reaction to *third nerve* situations? When manic (when *Sham* has been in the driver's seat) anger has been like dried kindling, and any spark has set it off in me. Moments of angry disruption have occurred numerous times in the past... such as the time when a brother was not able to attend my wedding—and I blew up,...when a banking hassle became a fiasco, and when I perceived favoritism at All Saints Catholic Church (the parish I attend), and I abruptly decided I no longer belonged there. To *Sham*, anger means separation and dismissal of crucial relationships—such as with Sandra in late summer of 2008.

### what anger

what is
this anger that boils red
like a screaming teapot inside

if it were
up to me I would
crush every can
in the face of
pitiful happiness
and slice to pieces
the fruit of the successful

it's obviously
an anger unmentionable
and yet inescapable

what anger
what

As you can see, my anger gets pretty radical, and pretty grim. *Sham* used this "screaming teapot" for his advantage last year. Annoyances became magnified beyond description, and steeped to a cool hatred, often undetectable. Sham kept it all inside, stewing over often-petty annoyances and lingering disappointments.

Now, my challenge is to take that energy and put it to good use. I'm relearning how to listen to, empathize with, and to praise others for "mini victories" that I notice. The other day, Sandra used my car and filled it up with gas on her return home. I found myself noticing the small detail and praising her for the loving gesture. This was a revived, if not new, behavior for me.

Anger has a way of filtering down to every aspect of life. But when headed off at the pass—by expressing it assertively—anger's energy can be transformed into compassion and hopeful responses. Recently, Sandra and I were discussing what we would do if someone cut us off on the freeway. We both responded that we would probably call the person a jerk—or worse. Then I proposed that we not focus on the person but the behavior, and choose to exclaim..."that was a dangerous move!" or "what rude behavior!" We both admitted it would take a lot of work to switch attitudes because we wanted to avoid labeling—just as we didn't want to hear others state "he's a bipolar" or "she's mentally ill."

It occurred to me today that "you gotta go with what ya got." It's the NIATI theme (Now Is All There Is)—an attitude that assists me in dealing with my anger. The more I realize and show gratitude for the small pleasures and kindnesses of others who are all around me, the more I will be spending my energy on positive outcomes, not on resentments and stuffing my anger.

I thank God for the *blessed distractions* that keep my mind on the positive—nurturing the good in others and myself---in my attempts to *Focus On the Good.*

# Chapter 15

## Improbable dream

Last night—or I could say, this morning—I had a dream. It was a strange dream, yet somehow it seemed so accurate, felt so palpable. I was a homeless man lying on the bright yellow, freshly painted handicapped ramp of a busy city street corner. People were buzzing by all around me, and I just laid there, in my sweatshirt, jeans and baseball cap, with a blanket pulled over me. The odd thing was that I didn't feel bad about it. I wasn't particularly enjoying myself, but I wasn't suffering.

In a number of ways, this image fits my life. Kind of odd, this being two days after I had an epiphany about a new purposeful venture in life—to begin a campaign of awareness about bipolar that promises to be quite eventful and fulfilling.

My "street dream" was a bit unrealistic though—I was not the ordinary street person. I was not hungry; I did not have to "use the facilities;" I was cleanly-shaven, and I was comfortable—lying there on the cement. What *did seem* accurate was that I didn't have anywhere to go, and I spent time just watching others go by. This dream had combined the contradictions and complexities of my present situation into an image I understood, but I had never imagined myself in that role before.

Could be scary stuff but it would have been even more scary living in a waking nightmare of not being in Milwaukee at all. I could still be back in Grand Rapids, Michigan, *Sham*-driven, sicker than ever—having never awakened from my manic state. This could easily have been my lot at this moment—other than God saw it another way. I would have surely run out of money by now and would most likely be living in my car.

"But for the grace of God go I" is a maxim stated in 12-Step meetings, and I find, at this point in my life, that this form of gratitude is extremely appropriate. I am multi-blessed to have made it back to Milwaukee, to have an understanding, loving wife, and to have a new, captivating mission in my life.

*You cannot discover new oceans unless*
*you have the courage to lose sight of the shore.*

*(motivational poster)*

Maybe the reason I was lying at the edge of the street in my dream was to simply find out what it felt like to be destitute, and that I wasn't there because the street was my new home. It was too clean, the accommodations too comfortable and my spirits too high for it to be a realistic permanent setting. So why the dream? What was it trying to tell me? I didn't feel discriminated against for having a mental illness… for some reason I fit in A-OK.

Although the dream depicted me as being clean, comfortable and well-fed, I see it as representing my present state of being "temporarily homeless"—seeking a roof over the head of my battered self-image. This is a time of transition, of huge change—but not of desolation or despondency. My bipolar has thrown me some curve balls and I DO feel sort of out of place—but not lost. So many others have it so much worse than I!

Yet life has been an emotional and intellectual rollercoaster since I returned to Milwaukee from Grand Rapids—coming home to Sandra and beginning the journey of writing this memoir. It has been quite a ride! It's amazing how having productive, steady employment grounds us, so much so that when it is absent, we can feel quite lost. My volunteer work has been the saving grace, (along with the loving kindness of Sandra), keeping me at least somewhat busy with productive ventures. These activities include serving the poor in our community and listening to others with mental health challenges on a support call-in line. I enjoy these activities, but until I get my public speaking career in full swing, I believe the uneasiness I feel will continue.

Sandra and I are starting up a business in which interactive public speaking is the main thrust. We call it *Authentic Journeys* and we will be giving presentations on self-esteem, bipolar, bullying and other important topics (www.authenticjourneys.org). We are currently working on creating our speeches & promotional literature, and are networking throughout the greater Milwaukee area. It's pretty exciting to be moving in this direction—certainly not like lying on a street corner!

One of the ways I have used time productively lately has been to work on a philosophy of life that I can use in whatever I do—whether in a paid job or volunteer work—or just as a set of personal guidelines. It has many hours to distill myriad ideas and concepts into the following—see what you think of it:

## The Integrity Code

### Achieving Interpersonal Excellence

### by Rich Melcher

*Let us look for the good in others and ourselves and,*

*in time, it is all that will catch our attention.*

*Each Day A New Beginning*

*Life is great when goodness meets goodness.*

*Rich Melcher*

## *Accepting*

- Showing sincere respect for others and ourselves by offering life-enhancing, non-judgmental attitudes and actions...
- Acknowledging and advancing others' and our own self-worth...
- Forming and honoring appropriate, healthy boundaries...

## *Connecting*

- Listening to others with focused attention...
- Communicating openly, honestly and assertively...
- Seeking the opportunity in every difficulty, rather than the difficulty in every opportunity...

## *Expressing*

- Creatively expressing our authenticity, while encouraging other to do the same...
- Offering appropriate, life-enhancing humor...

- Choosing to display our sincere gratitude consistently...

This is the abbreviated version of the philosophy. It took me over 100 hours to create this philosophy—a venture well worth ANY time put forth.

The Integrity Code is a culmination of my personal learnings over the past 30 years. It is a basic blueprint to guide my life—and will hopefully become a positive influence on the lives of those with whom I will share it.

Actually, it took from April to December, 2008, to create and revise (and revise again...and again) this Code. Surprisingly (and unknowingly) it kept *Rich* (the healthy me) in the picture when *Sham* (the ill me) was attempting to destroy my relationships and cripple my life. Writing and re-writing this philosophy connected me with my *Authentic Self* like nothing else (along with praying *the Rosary*).

I'm amazed at how God can put an idea, activity or person in our lives—at just the right time—that helps us keep afloat when times get rough! This philosophy was certainly one of those ideas—or group of ideas—and it shines a light on my wishes to teach about interpersonal communications in the future. But it's a good thing that God is in control, 'cause I never would have thought this one up on my own!

The *poet* in me sees this blessed creation of a life philosophy—that saved the ship from going down—as an improbable imperative, a blessing that hid in my Gateway computer for so many months (while *Sham* ruled), and a proclamation that came through to assist me in continuing my life as husband, church member, son, step-dad, volunteer, Christian man, and as poet . . .

# poet

what is it to be
poet
breeze flowing thru fingers
weeks and years of thoughts and feelings
found dancing descriptively in lines
of black & white
where distilled emotion
and focused images find home

poet

be poet
be who you truly are
far from scenes of
comparison and affirming glances
here—finding self
on the pages of the heart

poet

recognizing a soul breath
catching a thought-butterfly
then letting it fly free ~
exposed for all to see
yet only liberated thru catching the wind

poet

finds the simple

*and creates the important*
*where a mere observation*
*becomes an entire landscape~*
*here life comes alive*
*and fledgling artist*
*becomes*

*poet*

# Chapter 16

# Found

It may seem foreign to you that I've spoken of a man (me) split between a healthy and a broken personhood, but it has been quite real—and often surreal—for me. In the early 1970s, the original *Star Trek* had an episode (somewhat of a "manic episode") where Captain Kirk had been split into two separate people—a hyperactive, impulsive, explosively violent man, and a docile, unaware, nearly drugged-up man. They had to lock up the over-active Kirk, yet the docile Kirk was still expected to run the ship, and had great difficulties trying to make decisions. In my eyes, this represented a manic and depressive split—a bipolar imbalance!

The only way to get him back *interconnected*—to become one man again—was for the two "Kirks" to embrace and be sent out into "deep space" through the transporter, and beamed back to the ship—in hopes that this would make the two Kirks one man again. It was a huge gamble, but seemed to be the only option to get the assertive, productive, competent Captain Kirk back.

Sometimes I wonder if our destinies can be implanted in our psyches by such media influences. At the early age of 10, because of good ol' *Star Trek*, I had seen the potential for the possible re-integration of a person's "shadow" into the predominant personality. Viewing this past year's destructive events, I'm so extremely grateful that Jesus came to me and returned my lost sheep, *Sham*, because I cannot live without him.

You may be wondering, "*Cannot live without him?! After all the destruction and near tragedy Sham brought you?*" Yes. As you see, Captain Kirk was merely half a man when separated from his "Sham," the angry, hostile part of himself. But he couldn't function as leader without the gifts that came from these qualities—which brought energy and vibrant life to his personality. He needed his Sham, just as I need mine…the quirky sense of humor, the wild dreams of possible successes, the crafty scheming, the dramatic proclaiming. *(This is what I call "HRQ's": Highly Redeemable Qualities…even Hitler had the HRQ's of drive, enthusiasm and a charismatic speaking aura.)* My latent HRQ's have come back to me, but now I've acquired appropriate boundaries once again, which, when re-integrated within *Rich*, have allowed for a fullness of self. The split personality is gone! The alter-ego has gone back into the shadows!

Captain Kirk's risky re-integration experiment was a success in the *Star Trek* episode, and he came back through the transporter as himself—manic and depressed having been balanced into a happy, "well-adjusted" man.

> *Persons with high self-esteem feel a connectedness*
> *to their own inner drives, images and objectives.*
>
> *Marsha Sinetar*

In 1988, my mother and I viewed the movie *The Wiz* and were totally taken by it. The theme that most captured me was this idea of self-integration—bringing the disparate parts of ourselves together to form this Captain Kirk-like transformation. Unlike the original Wizard of Oz, The Wiz brought in spiritual elements such as *The Blues* to amplify the Scarecrow's "*trappedness*," the Tin Man's *brokenness*, and the Lion's *fearfulness*. I had related to all of these in 1988, and I relate to them even now. The difference is that my process of self-integration was begun in '88 and, although I haven't quite found home inside myself yet, I'm way on down that road!

In The Wiz, Glinda, the Good Witch of the South, had spoken of "home" to Dorothy. Dorothy replied, "Home? Inside of me? I don't understand!" Glinda continued, "Home isn't just a place where you eat or sleep, child…home is knowing…knowing *your* heart, knowing *your* mind, knowing *your* courage…when we know ourselves, we're always home—*anywhere*!"

In '88, I was a very insecure, unaware, confused young man. The concept of self-integration was brand new to me. But after 21 years of contemplating the state of my self-integration and consciously moving in that direction, I'm in a much better place. Even so, it has been such a shock to go through this explosive encounter in 2008, discovering that, indeed, I was NOT truly self-integrated, and discovering the influences of this newly-defined alter ego—*Sham*. It was a real blow to my ego to realize that, after all these years of trying to reach this HOME (this *interconnectedness*), it could be dashed on the rocks of manic flight in a flash, nearly destroying all of my most precious relationships! Here is a taste of how I have felt at many times:

### *believing in*

*having a hard time believing in*
*my self*
*who is this person*
*I cautiously look at in the mirror?*
*it's almost as if I were a foreigner*
*in a distant land*
*on unfamiliar—but fertile—soil*
*that promises no place to rest my head*
*nor tend my sheep on pastures*
*green yet unforgiving*
*with brooks babbling a forgotten tale*
*of who I once thought I could become*

*believing in*
*believing in*

*believing in myself is probably*
*the most difficult task I will ever encounter*
*especially since I seem to have so many disparate*
*parts of myself all inside this one heart, mind & soul*

*which ME am I to believe in and*
*which bloodied dream should I raise high*
*in this battle for pure understanding and embittering*
*pre-broken promises?*
*it is me I must believe in*
*but which ME and which way*
*do I choose?*

Bipolar is a cunning and devious taskmaster that, when unbalanced, can overcome an individual—either on the manic or depressed end of the spectrum. My own system has gone to the manic side three fourths of the time. Why? I don't know...possibly a combination of brain chemistry, personality type, and/or past experiences. But I am grateful that, even with all the messiness of sliding toward the manic side so often, I rarely suffer from chronic depression. When in depression, those have been the absolute worst of times!

Meeting up with the movie The Wiz was a huge GOD THING in '88 because, without its influence, I may have succumbed to an incognito *Sham* and his negative influences many years ago. Maybe I had been readied to become aware enough and strong enough to go through this past year's test. Not that Jesus was testing me, but that my life of hiding and pseudo-connecting with the inner-self had to come to a climax.

This is why I believe the recent *disappointment to transformation,* brought on by the Catholic men's conference, needed to happen for me to get back to a truer calling—to move toward speaking again to groups about bipolar and other important topics, and to become a positive force for change. Since I have been in Milwaukee these past four years, I have *never* spoken in public about bipolar, as I had done so often in Minnesota between 1992 and 2002. Like the Wiz' Scarecrow I've felt trapped, like the Tin Man broken, and like the Lion, fearful. But it's time for me to bust out of these constraints and "come into my own!"

THIS I choose to do!

This prospect of speaking excites me in a very different way than any type of writing. Speaking has an urgency and a "one shot at it"-element that brings adventure into the scene. I love that! It's this pull, this tension between experiencing the joys of speaking in public and the stressors of making it happen, that keep me going these days (that and my beloved Sandra's encouragement). I think and feel I could make a REAL difference in my community—yet struggle with that old familiar thorn—procrastination. But in the end, I believe my mission will overcome any mountain, and God's plan will prevail in all I do. God has been so very good to me.

## *the greatest feeling*

*the greatest feeling*
*is to be a part*
*of something much*

*bigger*

*than myself*

*something good*
*creative positive up-lifting*

*something involving much effort and energy*
*creating bonds between people and places*
*transforming me into an*

*indispensible component*
*calling out my abilities*
*exposing my talents*

*to be a part of bringing*
*life back to the lives of those beyond this skin exhilarates me*
*let it happen*
*let me play a part*
*a lead among many leads*
*Lord, give me, this day, my daily bread*

*my purpose*

*my identity*

# Chapter 17

# Encounters with Blackness

Yesterday, the day before Martin Luther King Day, as I stood in the choir before the All Saints Catholic Church congregation, I had a feeling. It was a feeling I hadn't had at all in 2008—probably not since I married Sandra at All Saints in October of 2007. Sandra and I had asked the choir to sing at our wedding, and the feeling of sharing our African-American Catholic church community (which is 70% African-American, 20% white and 10% African) with my Caucasian family thrilled me greatly. The feeling on our wedding day—and finally again yesterday—was the sense that *I belonged* . . . that I was valued by the people at All Saints, and that my spirituality was back on the right track. My spirituality was "born" (or re-born) in a black Catholic church—Holy Angels—when I first came to Milwaukee in 1984. So, this tradition and style of worship is very dear to me.

Sometimes it's difficult to tell where bipolar begins, and where it ends. How did I end up marrying a beautiful black woman? How is it that I have three wonderful black step-daughters? Why am I a member of a Black Catholic church? And what does this all have to do with my bipolar development? Everything!

Let's take a look back for a moment...I have a history with "blackness"... destiny/chance called as I was trying to figure out what to do after my college graduation, which was quickly approaching—in spring of 1984. My life took a blessed and crucial turn that shaped me in substantial and life-changing ways. Was it chance, or destiny—I don't know… as Forrest Gump would say, "I think it (was) both…both happening at the same time." I would say that God just knows the best way to bring out our best—our Best Selves.

My brother John suggested the Jesuit Volunteer Corps (JVC) as an option. Since I didn't know WHAT I wanted to do with my mass communications degree, I opted for *JVC: Midwest*, which met the needs of the disadvantaged in such cities as Chicago, Cleveland, Detroit and Milwaukee. I asked to be assigned to Milwaukee because it was the only city in *JVC: Midwest* that I had visited—and it was an enjoyable experience.

I was selected to be a physical education teacher at the aforementioned St. Leo's Grade School, in urban Milwaukee. I had NO IDEA what I was getting into! I remember walking into that classroom on the first day...12 faces staring at me—12 black children lookin' at this white guy, probably thinking, "Who is this dude?" or "Is he the new teacher?" Truth be told, I had only one black friend before walking into that school, but I soon had dozens of black students whom I admired. I fit in immediately! And because of my "personalizing" ways, my interests and even language style (at least during school time) moved toward **blackness**. Soon, I joined the Holy Angels Black Catholic congregation and their gospel choir. This was a good fit—an integrated congregation with a lively gospel choir.

I loved working at St. Leo's! It was the place where "*Teacher*" become one of my five favorite words. I never taught "physical education," (as was my initial job title) but became a math, English and reading teacher—well, *teacher's assistant*, to be exact.

The first real *connection* I had with my students came in October of '84 when I brought John Howard Griffin's Black Like Me in to read to my 5th grade math class. I was taking a risk by teaching literature in math class, but it paid off! Black Like Me is a true story of a white man who, in 1953, went to New Orleans and colored his skin brown, to see what it was like to live as a black man. The kids were amazed that anyone would do this—and so was I.

It wasn't very long after reading this that one girl looked up at me and said, "Mr. Melcher, you act black!" This proclamation was an honor, yet quite baffling. How can a white guy like me *act black?* But I had taken on some characteristics of blacks, including occasionally speaking some Black English, and displaying similar body language. So, I guess I fit in.

After the amazing year at St. Leo's, I did a second year with the JVC, this time at a small integrated Milwaukee high school. With little funding or materials, and no professional experience as a high school speech and creative writing teacher, I found myself in a very distressing situation. Part of my job was to recruit for this struggling school and it felt so phony. The worst part was that I was plugging for a school I didn't believe in, and, being an inexperienced volunteer teacher, **I** was part of what I didn't believe in—I was part of the problem. This is the exact definition of SHAME. *I was the problem!* (at least in MY mind).

That ethical dilemma, along with bursts of unresolved anger, led to my first hospitalization, releasing me from my responsibilities at the high school in February of 1986. It was a completely unbalanced year that included six hospitalizations, (four for mania and two for depression). After this first hospitalization, I left the Milwaukee high school position and went back to Minnesota.

Would you believe that my gold (my "black experience") became rust when I left Milwaukee? I went back to what I call the "www"...the wonder bread white world...Minnesota. Minnesota has few African-Americans, and my family didn't know how to deal with a loved one who talked about urban Milwaukee as if it were Heaven. I felt alone, isolated, depreciated. I felt I had no one to talk to about my experiences in the black culture or at Holy Angels, (the Black Catholic Church in which I had been a choir member) or even my wonderful days at St. Leo's! My world in Minnesota had never heard of gospel music in a Catholic church..."What? They clap their hands to the music? And play a tambourine? "

I remained in Minnesota for the next 18 years—with nearly no contact with blacks, except when I would go back to Milwaukee to see friends, every 5 years or so. In fact, my mind performed an amazing, self-protective act, in order to keep sanity in the picture...I unconsciously buried my "Milwaukee Self" in 1994 or so. I psychologically and emotionally buried my connectedness with the black culture—a destructive moment in my personal history, and a critical blow to my spirituality.

I had tried to connect with the only black Catholic parish in Minnesota and found it somewhat cold and regimented—nothing like Holy Angels back in Milwaukee. So, I believe my mind just repressed my experiences of St. Leo's & Holy Angels to safeguard my heart, mind & soul from the pain of the loss. No longer in existence. It "worked" for a while, until the "blackness in me" started **bubbling up** years later.

## integrity *bubbling up*

*funny how a guy can go for years and years*

**believing** *one thing (or, at least, believin' he's believin')*
*& suddenly past images surface*
*disappointment disillusionment disagreement*
*discouragement disregard*
*honor hope*
*gratitude*
*love*

*they all come*

**bubbling up**

*recently they emerged*
*like a shipwrecked seaman*
*who has cast his net upon me*

*and he is*
*ME*

*long-buried treasure—gold coins flung at the feet*

*this is the realization of true inner longings,*
*once-blanketed observations*

*this is ME*

*here to reclaim the fertile soil of my unkempt but dazzling soul*
*not as if a flag planted stiff on dusty lunar surface*
*but as oak roots strong*
*with a wide-reaching anchoring trunk*

*no longer a prisoner of a benign yet besieging lostness*
*that for so long kept the blinders and earplugs secure*
*no more*
*no more*
*lie uprooted & truth revealed*

The jail cell of my hidden "Milwaukee Self" was sprung wide open in May of 2005 when, in a manic state, I decided I needed to go back to "the city of my success" and packed a U-haul, heading for Milwaukee. I immediately joined All Saints Catholic Church and soon joined the choir. In 2006, I met Sandra at a copy shop where I was employed. Long story short, we fell in love and married in October, 2007. Marrying a wonderful black woman, and being blessed with three step-daughters and two step-grand daughters led my life in full-circle. My desire to "be a part of" the black community had come true—in ever-blessed ways!!

There are many places that I could place blame for the troubles I have had with my bipolar. But I believe that my connection with the African-American community in Milwaukee has been one of the greatest factors in bringing light into my life, and in bringing me back to myself. *Sham* didn't have problems with Sandra last fall on the account of her being black—she just happened to be near. And I didn't go down in flames at the Milwaukee high school in 1986 because of the contact I had with blacks, but just the opposite. It was the feelings of loss due to leaving the African-American community in Milwaukee that prolonged the emotional pain and disillusionment—resulting in a very unbalanced state.

Yesterday, the *FEELING* I got at church (mentioned earlier) was one of joy and connectedness—something I rarely felt in 2008, as I was mud wrestling with *Sham*...and it feels great to have it back!

One more thing about my first experiences at St. Leo's Grade School . . . before fall of 1984, I had little knowledge of or feelings for Martin Luther King Jr., or the Civil Rights Movement. It was those kids, those wonderful African-American grade schoolers who brought Dr. King into my life, and made him my hero! I am forever in their debt for this gift—one they never knew they gave me. God bless 'em!!

## King

Martin Luther King, Jr., was a *NOBODY*
when I was growing up
in that Minnesota
"wonder-bread-white-world"...
he was never mentioned ~
my world touted a deafening silence
hiding this man of PEACE
& gave me a John Wayne, a Tarzan
and an occasional Sidney Poitier
(in "*To Sir, With Love*")

but the children
my black students in urban Milwaukee
ahh---they taught me—
taught me you don't have to be
"black-skinded" to live a black theology
full of praise and joyful gospel sounds

*KIDS*...they don't know how to hate
until they're taught...and these glistening gems
obviously knew love & reached out to express it!

so, Martin, I can say with confidence
  and a healthy pride that,
    thanks to these kids, I've finally met you
      and made you a part of my family

# Chapter 18

## inner life

Through the years of struggle with bipolar, I have cultivated the idea—the belief—that self-esteem is an all-important inner-power. The speech below represents my deepest thoughts and feelings about the topic, soon to be presented in area schools and at community youth agencies. I hope you like what I have to offer.

## The Road to Self-Esteem

**(. . . This is an audience participation speech . . .)**

**You've probably heard the term self-esteem, right? This talk is called The Road to Self-Esteem because we all are on a path—a journey—to discover who we are, and hopefully to like what we find. In this talk, I will speak of ways you can have greater self-esteem and thus have a happier life.**

**So, what is YOUR definition self-esteem? (Audience Response = AR)**

**My definition of self-esteem has 3 parts:**

1) seeing the good in ourselves and valuing who we are,

2) having self-confidence and knowing that we are OK, just the way we are, &

3) being able to accept ourselves...the good and the not-so-good parts.

I call this having authentic self-esteem. Who can tell me another word for "authentic?" (possible AR = "real, genuine, true...") . . . Great! To be authentic means to be true to yourself—to be real—to be who you were meant to be! The opposite of authentic self-esteem is false self-esteem. Tell me, what—to you—is "false self-esteem?" (AR)

Very good! What I heard from you was...(summarize)...Let me add to that. I see false self-esteem is when others put on an act that they are confident, even though they are actually fearful and insecure. Many times these people end up being the bullies.

You know a bully when you see one...a bully shoves you around or calls you mean names or threatens to hurt you. Let me tell you—THAT person most likely has very low self-esteem. And the person who takes the abuse from the bully can also have low self-esteem...he or she often feels less-than because of the bully's cruel words and actions.

Also—something you may never have thought about before--false self-esteem comes from "thinking we ARE our grades." We all get grades—we've been getting grades since 1st grade, or so. But when we feel WE ARE our grades—this is trouble! When I was growing up, I saw myself as an "A- person." I got mostly high grades on tests and they were, on the average, A-'s. I breathed A-air, I had A- friends, I got an A- on my driver's test, and I had an A- attitude. In my head, I was "Mr. A-"!!

But during my senior year of high school, I got very depressed because of a mysterious illness, and, in my head, I became an "F person." I felt like an "F washout," and was getting F's because I wasn't doing the work! I went from what I thought was high self-esteem to low self-esteem—if not NO self-esteem!

We all have high self-esteem in some areas, and low in others. For me, I feel great when I write poetry, but feel kind of lousy when I balance my check book...good at writing—not very good at math! You see, self-esteem is not like a stone fortress that can never be moved or changed. It is more like a river that flows through our lives.

The trick is to keep the water flowing at an even rate. If the river of self-esteem rises too high, it can flow over its banks (like when someone who thinks they're better than others). Or if the river of self-esteem dries up, it becomes a dry river bed, (like when a person feels worthless and unlovable). Authentic self-esteem means to be confident, aware and hopeful.

To be honest, during all my middle school and high school years, I was the "goof-around kid." I was always trying to get attention, to get praise because I had low self-esteem half of the time. (This has often continued into my adult years). I did all kinds of silly things to get attention. I remember the time, when I was 10 or so, a friend dared me to ride my bike into a grocery store—you know, through the doors that open automatically! I was quickly ushered out by an angry employee! And at age 16, I tried to drive up a muddy hill with my two-wheel drive truck and got massively stuck in the mud! It took two 4-wheel drive trucks an hour to get me un-stuck! OOOOPPPSS!

The problem was that I really didn't know WHO I was—and I was always following the crowd. I had a great need for some guidance—someone to help me **value** myself—to see the good in me—to show me I COULD do something right. This was when something very important happened in my life.

I was 14 years old and it was our final practice of the year for my hometown hockey team. Minnesota is COLD in February, but my coach—Coach Peterson—pulled me aside to practice a particular skill with which I had been having difficulty.

As all my team mates headed off the rink, I stood in my skates—freezing cold—and took instructions from my coach on how to (as he put it) "take the man out of the play." This meant that, as an opponent approached with the puck, I was to get in his way—often forcefully—to keep him from moving past me. This sometimes meant knocking him down onto the ice! But I had been having a hard time with this skill, and often, players were just passing me by.

Coach Peterson had me skate backwards while he came at me with the puck...he darted left, then right...and left me standing there looking stupid! So I tried again, and this time he said, "Look at my stomach." When he came down the ice at me again, he faked me out of my skates! Then he yelled, "Watch my stomach! Go wherever my stomach goes, and take IT out of the play!"

One last time he came at me . . . I looked directly at his stomach, ignoring his stick, ignoring the puck, and when he tried his fancy stuff, (darting left, then right), I went toward him and took his stomach out of the play—and his whole body as well! I did it!! I had it!! There was no turning back once I KNEW how to take the man out of the play!

This came in handy a week later, on our hockey trip to Northern Minnesota, when I encountered an opponent roaring down the ice towards me. Skating backwards with my new skills on my mind, I focused on his stomach and hit him so hard that he flew up into the air and tumbled onto the ice! My teammates stood up and cheered, not knowing that I had it in me. Now they, as well as I, knew the truth—I HAD IT IN ME!

I learned how to *value* myself through those hockey experiences. I didn't have to be the goof-around kid when I played hockey after that—I had confidence—a confidence that spread into every area of my life. This is one way of gaining self-esteem—through our successes!

Think for a moment...what are YOUR successes? . . . . . Don't you know how GREAT you are?! I bet if I could just have a 10 minute conversation with each of you, I could tell you 10 things I like about every one of you! Everyone is interesting! Everyone is smart—in their own way! And everyone is blessed? So how could you be excluded? Don't sell yourself short!

I once heard of a kid who had no legs (you heard me!...no legs!)... and he tried out for the Minnesota Twins professional baseball team. He was out there "running" the 40-yard dash nearly as fast as the others (on his hands!) and chasing down fly balls like the rest of them. When asked why he tried out for the team, he simply responded, "Well, I had nothing to do until 3 o'clock!" What an awesome attitude, huh?! Just think of the image he had of himself going on inside his head. He could 'cause he thought he could!

Having a positive attitude toward yourself is all-important. But never forget that the good you have—the authentic self-esteem you've achieved—is to be given away...it must not be hidden inside. So how do you give your self-esteem to others? A little thing called "affirmation." To affirm another is to find the good in others AND TELL THEM! It means to give compliments, to encourage another in achieving a goal, to comfort a friend in a time of grief, or to welcome a new-comer.

The great thing is that when you affirm another, it soon comes back like a boomerang and you receive affirmation from them. Then you feel like giving even more the next time! And round and round it goes. That's how strong friendships are built.

What do you do to affirm others? How does it make you feel when you get a positive response back? Do you enjoy giving compliments? How often do you affirm others? (AR)

Giving back the good we've been given—this is what makes the world go 'round! We often learn how to value ourselves by the good things we do. But another very important kind of self-esteem comes from . . . how we *accept* ourselves—the good and the not-so-good parts. There are so many times in my life when I have made mistakes...do YOU ever make mistakes? Yeah, we all do! So what do you do when you make a mistake? How do you recover? When was a time that you made a mistake and had to make up for it? (AR)

Good examples! My feeling is that we must first admit we MADE a mistake. If we don't admit it, how can we correct it? When we do admit it, our self-esteem goes up a notch. When we learn from a mistake, our self-esteem goes up 10 notches because then we can avoid making the mistake the next time. When we can gain from our mistakes, we're on the road to success!

As the poet John Keats wrote:

Failure is, in a sense, the highway to success,
inasmuch as every discovery of what is false
leads us to seek earnestly after what is true.

*"Every discovery of what is false leads us to seek what is true!"* Exactly! We can gain from our failures, and achieve higher self-esteem, if we learn our lessons when they come our way.

When I was working at my dad's construction company many years ago, I made the mistake of driving a forklift onto a muddy surface. A forklift is a very heavy piece of equipment, and mud is very soft—and...well, YOU know what happened! . . . I got completely stuck! (sounds like I was always getting things stuck, doesn't it? Oh well...) I should have known I would get stuck! But I didn't. I learned—real quick—never to do that again!

I had to admit I had made the mistake because...well, because...I needed help getting the forklift out of the mud. Soon, all of my co-workers knew about my error and they had a good laugh—not with me, but at me. I felt pretty dumb. To raise my self-esteem again, I had to forgive myself for doing something so silly. I *accepted* myself for being a beginner and decided to let it go, learn my lesson, and move on. Sometimes we have to just keep movin' on down that road of life, you know?

So, to finish, I want you to remember the four very important ways of raising your self-esteem that we discussed today: (Now, I need a little audience participation...Repeat after me) . . .

1) We need to **avoid** the trap of false self-esteem,

2) We need to **value** ourselves for our many successes,

3) We need to **accept** ourselves when we make a mistake &

4) We need to **learn** our lessons as they come along!!

Excellent!! My challenge to you is to use these four tips, <u>and</u> find your own ways of raising your self-esteem because, when you think about it, the most important opinion you will ever have is the one you have of yourself . . . let me repeat that . . . *the most important opinion you will <u>ever</u> have is the one you have of yourself* . . . so why not seek to have a <u>great</u> opinion of yourself?... by pursuing authentic self-esteem!

If you do this, you will <u>surely</u> be on the road to happiness and success!!

# *Chapter 19*

# *Sham shame*

Life is funny. Not always the "Ha Ha" type, but often the "isn't that strange?" type. This morning was an example. While mixing up my chocolate protein drink, I closed the cabinet door, like usual, with a moderately loud "wham." Many of us probably do so and don't think a thing about it. But 25 years ago, I was MADE to think about it.

My awakening came while serving my first year in Milwaukee in the Jesuit Volunteer Corps in 1984. One of my housemates, (I'll call her Kelly), heard me "slammin' the cabinet doors" and angrily came in and confronted me on my "obnoxious behavior." In a red-faced shaming tone, she made it seem like I was a boor who was obviously out of line. Actually, I wasn't even conscious of my "slamming" and had no idea my actions were annoying her. I acquiesced to her insistence that I was rude and vowed to make every attempt NOT to slam the doors again.

But—funny how shame works—for these past 25 years, at least half of the time when I have caught myself slamming (closing) cabinet doors, the Kelly-incident would pop into my head, and I would feel self-consciously shameful. And I would often repeat "sorry Kelly!" under my breath.

When I closed the cabinet loudly this morning, Sandra didn't come running in to correct me, or to shame me…she didn't even notice. So, after whispering my, "sorry Kelly", I added, aloud, "but YOU don't live here!" It became clear that Kelly's sensitivity was just that—HER sensitivity…not my boorishness or insensitivity! And all these years I had beaten myself up over that!

Then, as if the fog was lifting, I realized how shame had played a destructive role on a much larger and more demeaning scale. I had encountered shame over how Kelly and all three of my other housemates in the Jesuit Volunteers had systematically rejected me and cut off all ties, after our year of living in community came to an end. It hit me that my former friends had not rejected me, *Rich*, but had really rejected *Sham*—the illness that had so often overcome me (although I had not yet identified or named *Sham*, and his unpredictable and inappropriate behaviors).

The yet-to-be-identified *Sham* was the one who left my housemates feeling uncomfortable after our Jesuit Volunteer community disbanded in 1985…*Sham* was the one who grew too attached to Denny... *Sham* was the one who hovered around Sienna and her new husband because of a lack of friends...and *Sham* was the one who ridiculously called Kelly "collect" in Pittsburgh for no good reason.

This realization that people react to my illness—to *Sham*—not to me, *Rich*, is extremely freeing!! The shame of *Sham* need no longer have this awkward and sickening tug on my stomach because I'm now choosing to recognize the shame-binders when they come in.

*If there is no enemy within,*
*the enemy outside us can do us no harm.*

*African proverb*

Letting go of my former Jesuit Volunteer housemates' responses to *Sham* is just the start of the self-forgiveness process. I don't need to hold on to such venom, based on shame that has distorted and contorted my life.

Now that I think about it, much of the shame I have experienced since my 1980 bipolar diagnosis has been due to either manic or depressive influences. Unlike *Sham* (of manic influence), depression—

represented by the term "depressive tendencies"—is more of a descriptor of negative feelings and attitudes. I have never become psychotically depressed, (if there even is such a thing). My understanding is that psychosis is a state of being so sick that you don't really even know who you are anymore. *Sham*...psychosis?—yes . . . *Rich*, my *Authentic Self*, has been the victim of *Sham's* psychosis!

**Shame** has been mentioned many times in this book, but I want to make one thing perfectly clear . . . shame is the enemy! To me, shame—this feeling that "I am the problem"—has killed more hours in my life, sent me into misery, self-doubt and self-pity more often, and clouded up more sunny days than ANY other single factor in my entire life!

Sometimes it was shame piled upon me, like with Kelly's "slamming." But most of the time it has been MY interpretation of how others were reacting—shame put upon me BY MYSELF! This type of shame is the worst because I'm always readily available to defeat myself—don't need cabinet doors or annoying-a-friend to do so.

Occasionally, over the past three decades, family and friends have said to me, "Rich, you're so hard on yourself!" This was like spraying vinegar in my eyes because I didn't understand what they meant, but I knew it wasn't a compliment. Now I know what they were talking about. Shame...self-shaming! I have had an incredible ability to find a way to feel bad about any given situation. It's not easy to admit this, but I believe it is true. Not that I did this with every situation—no. But when my buttons were pushed—such as about reading ability or competence in finances—I have often immediately felt the warm face and burning ears of my shame reaction.

I think what happened with the cabinet doors this morning, in all its innocent simplicity, is one of the greatest gifts God has EVER given me. Wow! To finally see, to taste, to touch the beauty of grace granted me in discovering how shame has bound me—and that it no longer has to do so! This is what I call a "life changer," and I can see how it can be lived out immediately.

First, it calls forth the fallacy I've carried for so long—that I need to feel bad about "*that which I have not done*." This is a mind-twister that I've grappled with furiously in my struggle to read more effectively. It's been a long hard road in this battle for my intellectual competency, but I now see that holding on to regrets over lost chances to read can only hurt me. So I let go.

Next, I can now drop the fallacy that the more I practice something, the worse I get—that I will just implant and imprint further bad habits. This might sound all backwards and inside out, but, at times, this lie has intruded and ruled over certain areas of my life. Giving speeches is my most prevalent example. I usually have no problems *writing* a speech, but when it comes to practicing it, I have often shut down, choosing to "wing it" rather than put in the effort to practice and perfect the speech.

This lie of "*practice makes problems*" came from my piano lesson days, grades 7 through 9. In my family, Melchers were required (by my dad) to play piano for 3 years and my "sentence" started in $7^{th}$ grade. I despised it! I came to hate practicing with a passion, and felt the more I practiced, the worse I got. I have known for years that "this was where self-hatred was born in my life." I felt I was wasting my father's money, and every moment I avoided practicing was like plunging a knife into his back, twisted by my defiant "faking like I was practicing." With this poor attitude in motion, I never put a full effort into playing piano. So, shame had a front door into my life—and I still live with the repercussions. But I now see that it's time to forgive myself, dust myself off and go on!

*We can learn to soar only in direct proportion to our determination to rise above the doubt and transcend the limitations.*

*David McNally*

Another way that shame has impacted my life is the tendency to keep alive old memories of all my goof-ups caused by inattention… the minor car accidents, the near-dangerous situations working at my father's construction company, the clumsiness. Problem is, I have often immortalized them as a part of my persona. Dangerous thing to do! Why dangerous? Because what one pays attention to tends to reoccur. If I <u>think</u> I drive recklessly, and focus on past failures, it is more likely that I will see myself as an unsafe driver and perpetuate my inner stereotype by getting into accidents. This type of thinking has never been a friend, but thanks to self-pity, it became my default setting.

Enough already! Self-acceptance <u>IS</u> my choice now! I know I will have to keep myself from "shaming myself," and learn how to re-direct any shame-based responses into more positive channels.

There is a new joy within me, though, as I see how this new freedom will affect my life. It's as though I'd been trapped beneath the ice and suddenly I've broken through the surface, gasping for the air of inner-peace and seeking the warmth of a heart released from a great burden. Thank God for breakthroughs!

## <u>conversion experience</u>**?**

no

i haven't been converted

black to white
doubt to trust
hate to love
cold to hot
despair to joy
dark to light

cataracts cleared
i now see what
was already
there

wash clear waters wash
clean the mud

from my eyes

blind man cried
*Jesus! Jesus! Let me SEE!!*

Your faith has healed you

now I see "me"

# Chapter 20

## tell it like it is

It's difficult to distill 30 years of knowledge and experience into a 25 minute talk, yet after all my efforts in writing speeches on bipolar, the final version is complete. I plan on giving this talk to youth and adults in the up-coming months. What do you think?

## bipolar balancing act

Jamal is a junior in high school, and for over a year he has had bouts of depression that made him sluggish, tired and feeling worthless. Then he would go on the up-swing and become excitable, energetic, creative and talkative. But, inevitably, he would gradually fall back into depression again. The cycle repeated over and over. He had no idea what was wrong, but finally his school counselor convinced him to get it checked out. After some tests, he was found to have a fairly common illness called bipolar disorder. Have you ever heard of it?

It's a hidden illness that affects 1% of the population. That means, if you go to a basketball or volleyball game, one out of every one hundred people around you will have this illness. It can be a devastating illness that can cause extreme emotional pain and behavioral upheaval. Yet it's silent and devious.

In this talk I am going to describe bipolar disorder to you, and the thoughts, feelings and behaviors that are created by the illness. Why? So, if spotted, you can help yourself or another get assistance. I am also going to speak with you about what I call the ABC's of Healthy Living, helpful guidelines for living a healthy, balanced life. To do so, I will use my personal experiences with bipolar disorder as a backdrop.

Bipolar Disorder used to be called manic-depression, but I'm just going to refer to it as BIPOLAR. So, what exactly IS bipolar?

*Bipolar is a hereditary*
*chemical imbalance in the human brain*
*that can cause dramatic mood fluctuations*
*and behavioral disturbances.* (repeat)

Bipolar can affect brain function when the brain chemicals are not balanced. This balance determines how you think and feel—and therefore, how you act. The illness is characterized by its manic and depressive symptoms:

~the depressive symptoms include feelings of worthlessness, decreased energy, loss of interest in activities previously enjoyed, loss of ambition and loss of enjoyment of physical activity...

~the manic symptoms include quite the opposite . . . increased energy, heightened creativity, rapid thinking, inflated self-esteem, rapid speech, elated feelings, impulsive over-spending and increased desire for physical activity.

I was diagnosed with bipolar 29 years ago and have had numerous struggles trying to control the illness! Since, as I mentioned, bipolar becomes active in over 1% of the population—often emerging in the late teens—I believe it's <u>very</u> important for you to know some details about the illness. Don't you? And what better way to learn than from someone who has it—right?

This is my "bipolar globe"… I created it to show exactly how bipolar works. The bipolar globe has 3 main areas—the orange stripe around the middle represents the "balanced" emotions… the yellow band above it represents the normal "happy" emotions that all people encounter, and the black stripe below represents the normal "sad" emotions we all experience. See how the upper arrows go up toward the North Pole (manic), and the lower arrows go down toward the South Pole (depressed)? This is why it's called "BI – POLAR"! With bipolar, the moods tend to move from feeling unrealistically good to feeling extremely bad.

The orange one inch wide stripe (which travels around the equator) shows the balanced feelings—when we're feeling good—not up and not down. But some events make us rise into the two inch wide yellow band—the excited, happy emotions; you know, like getting a well-deserved "A", or when our team wins a big game. At other times, we move into the black band—our emotions kind of take a dive, like if a pet dies or if we injure ourselves and can't participate in regular events for a time. Together the orange, the black and the yellow areas are in the NORMAL range of emotional experience.

But people with bipolar seem to have a broken regulator… do you know what a "regulator" is? Well, the regulator in this room keeps the room feeling comfortable. It regulates how the temperature increases and decreases. If it were broken, it may become very hot or very cold in here. For those who have bipolar, the emotions can fluctuate dramatically, and often unpredictably—sort of like having a broken regulator…the emotions can become "too happy" (manic) or "too sad" (depressed).

Without proper medications to balance the brain chemicals, a person with bipolar can be left in a very dangerous situation. The fluctuations in mood can make life chaotic and very unpleasant. These fluctuations don't usually happen every 10 minutes, or even every 10 hours. But there is such a thing called "mood swings" where the moods go between mania and depression uncontrollably. Mine usually take a number of days to swing—put they have been known to switch instantly, too. My mood swings occur when my medications are not balanced properly.

When did I realize I had bipolar? I didn't—at first. You see, it was January of 1980, (29 years ago)—my senior year in high school—when I first fell into depression. I had been having some unexplainable anxiety around Christmas, but one night in late January, I went to bed and started worrying . . . I began to think, "I don't think I'm capable of loving my parents,...and if I can't love my parents, how could I ever love my 8 brothers and sisters,...and if I can't love them, then what about my friends...?"—and on and on and on,...inside out and backwards. Within 30 minutes I fell off the cliff of despair, landing on the rocks of fear, regret and self-pity. I FELL..."bzzzzzzzzzzup----bam!"...into depression. The worst part was that I blamed myself because I had no idea I had bipolar, OR even that bipolar existed!

I suffered with depression for five months. Then, after graduation from high school, my moods leveled off and then soon began to rise! I became happy, energetic, creative, and talkative again! Eventually, I experienced all of these to the extreme! Without knowing it, I had risen beyond the yellow band of normal happiness and into mania! It felt great—opposite of depression...but there was certainly something wrong—something I couldn't detect. But my mom noticed the extreme changes and encouraged me (forced me) to get it checked out. That's when I was diagnosed with bipolar and went on meds immediately. Soon, the extreme moods faded, and I was at least in the lower yellow range again... more balanced—not so hyper or over-excited.

From these and other experiences with bipolar, I have developed the "ABCs of Healthy Living"...A-B-C being an acronym that stands for three extremely important components for living a healthy life...(poster)...Awareness, Balance and Connection. The ABC's of Healthy Living pertain to everyone, but in this speech, I'm going to focus on recovering from bipolar difficulties.

First we have Awareness! **AWARENESS** . . . since I live with bipolar, it's crucial for me to have what I call "$I^3$"...Insight Into my Illness...this actually goes for ANY illness. We need to know about the symptoms & treatments, the ins and outs of living with an illness, whether it be bipolar, cancer, MS or whatever. We need to have "$I^3$"...if we keep ourselves in the dark, we are at great risk of not being able to recover from the disease.

Not knowing the facts about bipolar during that 1st depression my senior year in high school put me at a great disadvantage because I often took it out on myself...I was confused, I began finding comfort in food—gaining all kinds of weight—and went downhill for 5 months, eventually coming to believe that taking my own life was the only way out.

After being diagnosed, I was on the road to becoming more AWARE of the symptoms of depression & mania. I finally had a fighting chance at staying healthy. The medications, the talk therapy, the support from my family and friends...these all made a huge difference in coping with the illness. Awareness is critical—awareness is the first step in understanding and dealing with any complex aspect of our lives.

Next, we have the "B" of the ABC's of Healthy Living . . . **BALANCE!** For a person with bipolar, life is like being on a high wire at the circus...tilting back and forth on that thin little wire. Tell me, what does a guy need when balancing on a high-wire? What does he hold in his hands?

Right! . . . a balancing bar. Everybody needs a balancing bar. A balancing bar consists of the healthy attitudes and activities that make all of our lives workable and enjoyable.

*So, what is one component of your "balancing bar"?*
*(Another way to put it is...What keeps you performing at your very best?)*

*Why do you think it's important to live a balanced life?*
*(What does "balanced" mean to you?)*

*If you could have ANY quality or skill you want, what would it be? Why?*
*Would it help you be a more balanced person? Is that important*

*to you?*

I **BALANCE** on that bipolar high-wire. Keeping balanced involves having a balancing bar with two distinct sides. First are the four fundamental physical components... these are important ways of taking care of the body:

- diet
- sleep
- exercise &
- medications

Then, on the other end, there are the personal essentials, the social-emotional areas of life:

- keeping a hopeful, optimistic attitude
- building connections with others
- respecting and expanding the spiritual life &
- exploring and developing important interests

I believe my balancing bar is pretty universal—is this how to stay up there on the high wire, performing the balancing act of your unique circumstances? Everything on my personal balancing bar is important, but I have found two components to be absolutely non-negotiable when dealing with my bipolar...can you guess what they are? One is pretty obvious—the one that actually stabilizes my brain chemistry . . . which one's that? Right. Medications. Can you guess the other?

Turns out to be . . . sleep. Why do you think sleep is so important? I mean, can't everyone just pull a few "all nighters" and be OK? For me, that's flirtin' with disaster.

Let's look at a computer analogy. The body is like the hardware—the computer itself. The brain is like the software . . . and medications keep the computer programs running properly. Sleep is like the power source. With bipolar, when I pull out the power cord and run on the battery, (in other words, go without sleep), the power doesn't last very long. When my sleep is shortened from 8 hours per night to 6, "the lights begin to go out upstairs." When I get only 4 to 5 hours per night, the software starts malfunctioning! And, with even less sleep, my medications stop working properly, and the software can be switched to an entirely different program.

Because I've had bipolar for 29 years, the illness has advanced so that I don't have "happy happy" manic episodes very often anymore . . . instead I can go into an angry, resentful, deceitful state. Here's a real-life example . . . let me introduce *Sham.*

Have you ever heard of an "alter-ego"? This is when someone has sort of a . . . separate personality. It's kind of like having a virus in the computer that plays with how the main program works. *Sham* is my alter-ego—this sneaky computer virus. He's a separate personality that comes out when my medications are not balanced <u>and</u> when I'm not getting enough sleep. *Sham* is the "ill Rich" coming out to play. Last year, *Sham* came out to play "BIG TIME". Inside my head, I was often bouncing from *Rich* (the healthy me—me right now) to the ill me—*Sham.*

Let me explain it from the viewpoint of a pilot...at these times, *Rich* (the healthy me), who is flying the plane, is attacked by *Sham,* dragged behind the pilot's seat and bound and gagged. *Rich* can still sort of hear and see what is going on but can do nothing about what *Sham* does in the pilot's seat. And *Sham* is generally angry, a big spender, resentful and full of unrealistic fantasies. Not a good situation!

After 29 years with bipolar, you'd think I would have gained some pretty good "$I^3$" ...Insight Into my Illness. But 2008 was an extremely disturbing year up on that high wire because of an event that hung a bucket of sand on one end of my balancing bar. In September of 2007, three weeks before my wedding, my doctor pulled me off all of my Lithium—the mood stabilizer I had been taking since I was 1st diagnosed back in 1980----my wonder drug for 28 years! Why? Because he suspected it was harming my kidneys.

No, I don't want to go on kidney dialysis—that's what my doctor feared. But by taking away this med so abruptly, it sent me spinning immediately into an upward manic spiral. I was talkin' fast and actin' fast and spendin' tons, and became ultra-creative, and was...just "not myself." That was the easy part!

I never did swing deeply into the depressive mode, but throughout 2008, swung between my main program—*Rich,* and the computer virus—*Sham.* The medication deficiency created a situation where sometimes I was just me, *Rich,* (creating positive projects and making friends)...then suddenly my personality would switch to *Sham,* filled with anger, destroying relationships—especially annoyed and destructive with my primary relationship—my wife!

Because of some blessed circumstances, I have reconciled with my wife, and have made up with my family—but that's only because I had become aware of the third component of the ABC's of Healthy Living . . . **CONNECTION**!

In 2008, I became disconnected from my support network—my wife, my church, my family and friends...I became VERY isolated, having NO CLUE that I was sick! The odd thing about mania is that the one in mania is the last to know it! It hides—totally! Do you think I would have left my loving wife last year if I had KNOWN what I was doing? It wasn't that I was out of control, but that *Sham* had control over me!

I must emphasize here the importance of building a strong support network. Making these connections with people and resources is probably one of the most important things you will ever do.

*Do you have at least one friend that you can really trust—someone with which you can share anything and everything?*

*Do you have at least one adult you could go to if you were really having a problem?*

Social connections are crucial! You know the great feeling when you make a new friend, or when you get together with a favorite aunt or uncle, or join a new group or team that brings out your best? Our connections with people are what bring life to Life! Some may say they are life itself!

Having bipolar, I have found it extra important to have plenty of friends and loved ones for two main reasons:

1) If I get depressed, I tend to isolate. It is very important at these times to have understanding, loving people around to support me and bring "the best out in me." Having others who care, and with whom I can share, protects me from getting down and in the dumps,

~ and ~

2) If I become manic, and especially if my *Sham* alter-ego comes out of hiding, I have people in place who will help me see that something's wrong—early on—before the illness takes over my life.

I truly believe that, no matter what troubles you may be having in your life, there is <u>always</u> hope! There are <u>always</u> people out there who can help you, and no situation is so grim that it can't be turned around! Look at me, for example . . . although bipolar had me in its grips just last year, HERE I AM!! And I've never been better.

That's because I'm open to learning life's lessons and I've been graced with the gift of persistence, to help me make it through. Also, I've been graced with the gifts of **AWARENESS**, **BALANCE** and **CONNECTION**, that create the simple formula that helps me in every area of my life . . . the ABC's of Healthy Living! I hope this formula has been helpful to you also!

*So, what's an important awareness that has come to you through this speech—what did you learn?*

*And, what's the most important human connection in your life? Why is this person important to you?*

*How could you help someone you know if you noticed the symptoms of depression or mania in them?*

*Do you now have a better understanding of bipolar than when we began?*

With bipolar, there's nothing to be afraid of. If a person has proper medications, a good "balancing bar," and a great support network, he or she can live a very happy and successful life.

I'm glad I had the opportunity to share this with you today!

# Chapter 21

# Validation

Crisp February 2009 afternoon; sun on my forehead; out walking for my prayer time…didn't get past the first bend when *The Wiz* came to mind. I heard in my heart's ear, the words of Dorothy…"*Is there a way I could find home*?" In 1988, when I first saw the movie The Wiz, the African-American version of The Wizard of Oz, I began the search for what I call self-integration. The Wiz modeled the process perfectly... Dorothy discovering three friends who represented her hopes and fears.

Self-integration means, to me, discovering the various parts of myself and inviting them to be unified within. Today, as I took my walk in the new-fallen snow, I asked God, "*Is there a way for me to come home?*" Self-esteem has been something I have struggled with sooooooo much in my life...plagued by feelings of inferiority and insecurity—often having NOTHING to do with my bipolar illness. It all comes back to *the Northern Lights*. Let me explain.

In the fall of 1982, I stood in the yard of the house I was renting and became distracted by something flashing above me. Looking up, I witnessed the most amazing cosmic scene—the midnight darkness brought bright lights bursting in from all sides, crashing into a center point…burst after burst! At first I had no idea what it was—like some strange rapid fireworks show, or something.

Then it hit me…it was "the Northern Lights"—a celestial phenomenon that appears in the northern sky. I had seen the Northern Lights in northern Minnesota years before, which had looked like broad waves of pale yellow light rolling across the sky as if some strange cloud formation. But THIS! This was something other! The brightness, the stark white flashes—I was witnessing what seemed to be a unique cosmic event!

After watching in amazement for a moment or two, I made one of the most life-directive and sadly future-revealing moves of my life. I thought, "I've got to share this with someone!" I remembered that six of my college buddies lived eight blocks to the north, so I threw on my roller skates and began skating up the road. When I got to their place, not only were my friends gone, but as I looked up in the sky, the Northern Lights had faded to nearly nothing! I had skated while they faded, and one of the most memorable moments of my life had been cut short by my "need to share."

What does this have to do with The Wiz and inferiority and self-integration? Well, everything! While I was on my walk today, I acknowledged that my self-esteem had been wavering due to being unemployed and the disillusionment that comes with it. A number of steps down the road, I began a conversation with myself:

> "In the Wiz, what was the Tin Man's gift?...Oh yes... emotional stability. How could I get more emotional stability in my life?"
>
> I continued my walk in the snow. Then it hit me…"D-TIP: *Don't Take It Personally!* I came up with that acronym in 1994 and, in 2008, I still took things too personally! If I were to stop taking things so personally, I bet this would give me more of Tin Man's *emotional stability*! Emotional Power! Good!
>
> "What about Scarecrow's intellectual capacity?" (I kept walking). "Oh! 'COLA!! Choosing Optimistic Loving Attitudes'! I came up with THAT acronym two weeks before D-TIP, and it's been a big help over the years…let's see,...*CHOOSING* Optimistic Loving

*ATTITUDES*...this is all about thinking and how to use your head. This could help with my 'Scarecrow intellectual capacity!' Thinking Power! Excellent!"

At that moment, I began to wonder, "*Why are all these acronyms coming to mind?...Oh well........*So what about courage and motivation?" I contemplated the Lion's lack of courage as I crunched through the snow.

Suddenly a new acronym I had created only 3 days earlier popped into my head..."FOG: Focus On the Good! Focus On the Good!! That's all about gaining more of the Lion's courage and motivation! Acting Power! Fantastic!! These are my three new companions...feeling power, thinking power and acting power!.......but...what does this all mean?"

I came to the mid-point of my walk, and, as I turned around, said to myself, "In The Wiz, Dorothy had questioned, 'Home—inside of me?! I don't understand!'...Well I don't get it either, God! How could **home** be i n s i d e m e e e . . . . . no . . . . . it couldn't be that simple!"

In the 20 degree weather, I quickly reached into my wallet and pulled out a double-sided, laminated business card imprinted with 32 of my personally-created acronyms...at the top was..."COLA: Choosing Optimistic Loving Attitudes"!!

I had been **"sitting on my wisdom**—my truth**"!!**—the card lying dormant in my wallet for 10 years! I had rarely pulled it out to scan how *I* view life and how *I* have made sense of my world. And why? Because I didn't believe others valued my acronyms. I had placed 7 or 8 of them in my first published book, years ago, and no one ever commented on them. I figured others just didn't give a rip about them. So why should I?

When I got home from my walk, I called Sandra into the den and, emotionally expressed, "All my life I have tried to get validation from others, to get others to like me, to be understood!" I reminded her of the story of my Northern Lights experience in '82, which I had shared months earlier...the "NEEDING others" to witness an event for it to be REAL to me. "I don't need others to approve of me" I exclaimed, "as long as I approve of myself! These acronyms are MY truth, and only I need to validate myself to be happy!"

*Amazing grace, how sweet the sound*
*that saved a wretch like me*

*I once was lost, but now am found*
*was blind, but now I see!*

*John Newton*

Because of that enlightening experience, I realized that I no longer had to look for HOME outside of myself. Although others may not value my acronyms the way I do (even though I had kept them hidden for so long) all that matters is that I feel they are valuable!

It's nice to get a pat on the back, or a smile, or kind words, but my creativity need not be judged by anyone but me. And I happen to like what I create!

Back tracking for a moment,...just before completing my walk, I began to think, "What are three words I can use to motivate myself—with my new mind, heart and courage?...'mind,' hmmm,...I have a creative mind. Yes, creative. 'Heart'? Hmm,...I'm ***passionate***... Great! Creative, Passionate...But what about 'courage'? Action. Movement. Oh, I know! In order to keep my sanity, to 'not *lose my mind*,' I need **focus**, like...*Focus On the Good*! That's it!"

This can be a true motivating force in my life. It has real meaning to me because it represents my new home, the real me, my *Authentic Self*. *Creative Passionate Focus* IS what I need to continue on this journey of living with the devastating illness of bipolar. And on I will go!

*to be*

*prove*
*move to*
*improve*

*never again trying to be something*
*for someone else*
*but only trying to be*

*to be*
*my best self*

Johnnie Colemon, Ph.D., writes that "There is no spot that God is not!"—truly a maxim I have tried to get across in *Discerning Bipolar Grace.* Through it all, especially this extraordinary past year of 2008, I have been blessed that the illness did not kill me, a family that did not abandon me, and learnings about an alter-ego (*Sham*) that no longer has power over me!

It was this completely messed up year of 2008 that showed me that I CAN make it through ANY tough time. These experiences have added many new layers of confidence to the candle I now choose to shine brightly. If not for bipolar, I would not be the man I am today; if it were not for bipolar, many of my creative ventures would never have been ventured; and if it were not for bipolar, I would never have learned that we all live with a gift and a curse—and it's all a matter of what we do with it!

From a little blond 8-year-old boy sitting in the sun, listening to The Carpenters and, unknowingly, discovering the gift and curse of "personalization," to a 46-year-old man out on a snowy walk suddenly realizing how his own acronyms held the answer to seeing that self-validation was the key, God has brought me to the throne of His Grace, time and time again.

# *Chapter 22*

## *prospects*

They say "hope runs deep"...this is my stance in my recovery from bipolar mania. It has been through writing Discerning Bipolar Grace that much of my healing has occurred in the past seven months, and a new vision has arisen. Never before in my life have I been blessed with such hopeful prospects. I acknowledge the numerous social and spiritual graces that have come my way...major steps in emotional intimacy with Sandra, re-entering the graces of my family of origin and step-family, my return to the All Saints Gospel Choir (which has returned me to my spiritual roots), and my ever-growing relationship with Mother Mary—enriched by praying *the Rosary*. I've been blessed in ways that I never dreamed possible, after all the turmoil of last year (the infamous 2008!) . . . the awarenesses, the potential speaking and constant writing opportunities, the good health, the balanced moods, and the kindnesses of family and friends.

I often wonder how I could be so blessed to have come out of the steep dive I experienced in 2008, and rise higher than I ever have before. Now, I'm not experiencing a "manic rise," a *Sham*-driven high, but a natural rise toward a more empowered self-image, a more optimistic viewpoint, and a stronger grasp on how to cultivate healthy relationships.

This morning, I pulled a blue 20-year-old sweatshirt from my closet donning its old familiar quote by Joseph Campbell:

## *Follow Your Bliss*

*If you follow your bliss*
*you put yourself on a kind of a track*
*that has been there the whole while,*
*waiting for you,*
*and the life you ought to be living*
*is the one you <u>are</u> living.*

Incredible timing! I needed to be reaffirmed that I am exactly where I'm supposed to be. My volunteer schedule is filling up with writing speeches, books and poetry...plus I'm scheduling gigs to speak in Milwaukee, and establishing *Authentic Journeys* with Sandra—our fledgling communications consulting business.

Speaking of spirituality, it has been a surprise to me that I am steadily becoming a more "religious" man—coming closer to my Catholic faith than ever before. Many people, I believe, see Catholicism as some kind of a relic, a holdout from a past theological tradition that has no relevance in today's society. I see it as exactly the opposite. To me, being a Catholic means having a grounding in the *original church* of the Christian faith, with a ceremony (the Mass) that has such depth, richness and tradition that—if one knows its significance—it is exceptionally beautiful and meaningful. Plus, I have the advantage of worshiping in a Black Catholic community—where "my spirituality was born" when I first came to Milwaukee in 1984.

I'm so very blessed! I don't have *everything* I want, but my life is opening up before me! I see it as "making a good thing out of a bad thing"—the old "lemons to lemonade" process. My rejection of Sandra, my family of origin and my step-family was probably months—if not weeks—from being a permanent loss last September, but God saw fit for the miracle of reunion and forgiveness to be a gift in all of our lives.

I tear up often when I reflect on this gift of family—loved ones who recognized that I was "not myself" and saw beyond the illness...who believed in *the real me* and welcomed me back...sort of a *Prodigal Son* occurrence. And it has been a blessing to chronicle this metamorphosis of the love I've been given—before, throughout and after the 2008 debacle.

## *what does it mean*

*in these days of hurry and often-glaring rudeness*
*what does it mean*
*to have family*
*to share LIFE with?*

*it means that no one goes hungry in the heart*
*no one goes thirsty from an unfed mind*
*no roofless tenants shiver in the soul*
*and no one abides in broken down shacks of withered personality*

*I love being loved by the ones I love*
*and I love loving those I treasure so dearly*
*it's as though God has matched us all up*
*to be there for each other in ever-special ways*

*I see it as a poignant and fruitful notion*
*that it was all supposed to be this way somehow*
*that family is meant to be something special*
*and even when separated we're only a heartbeat away*

*isn't it amazing the feelings realigned*
*the time melted away*
*and the hope renewed like a running stream*
*when we get together and see eye to eye once again?*

*God bless the family that never forgets*
*the gift given in a smile, a hug, a kiss*
*the Presence offered and received*
*whenever we as family come around the bend once more*

In 2008, God brought me through the loss of the life coach dream that brought chaos, a nasty manic state that nearly wiped out all of my relationships, and an emotional breakdown that put me in the hospital.

But, in 2009, God has graciously presented me with a walk in the snow that re-introduced the importance of self-validation into my life, the love of a wife who has accepted me back into her life, and many times of contemplation while writing this book that have given me crucial awareness and invaluable understandings about how 2008 turned out to be so destructive. I truly believe God whispers our truth to us, in so many ways, if we but listen and take heed.

In his book, Letting God, A. Philip Parham wrote: "*There is no power stronger on earth than the courage to face our past.*" Discerning Bipolar Grace represents my attempt to do just that. Yet not merely to face my past, but to create my future. Writing is a process of discovering, uncovering and recovering, and I have been amply blessed with this "podium of the pen" to air my struggles, triumphs, stories and wonderings.

I'd like to share this story, as told by Fr. Anthony de Mello:

*A man in India was walking into a village one day when he spotted a Sinyahsee (kind of a spiritual wanderer who saw the sky as his roof, the forest as his walls and God as his protector...so he just wandered from village to village, as the breeze blows a dried leaf).*

*The man grew very excited upon seeing the Sinyahsee and ran up to him, calling out, "Give me the stone—give me the precious stone!"*

*"What are you talking about?" said the Sinyahsee.*

*"I had a dream last night," said the man, "and in it God Himself told me ...'you will see a Sinyahsee in the village tomorrow, and if he gives you the precious stone he has, you will be the richest man in the world!' ...Do you have the stone?"*

*The Sinyahsee rummaged around in his satchel and pulled out a huge diamond—the biggest diamond in the world!*

*"Oh!! Will you give it to me?!" cried the man.*

*"Sure," said the Sinyahsee, "I found it in my travelings—I think in a forest somewhere." How great was the man's surprise and his joy!*

*Being the middle of the day, the Sinyahsee walked on and sat under a tree, to get out of the hot rays of the sun. The man, too, sat beneath a nearby tree to ponder his treasure. He thought for hours and hours. In time, his face changed from a glowing smile to a calm seriousness.*

*Then, as the sun was nearly setting, the man got up, slowly walked over to the tree where the Sinyahsee was sitting, carefully handed the diamond back to the Sinyahsee and said:*

*"Here...I don't want this diamond . . . but could you give me the riches*
*that make it so easy for you to give this thing away?"*

Oh, the many riches that lie within us, if we were to but search into the vastness of our minds and hearts for the treasures of inner-peace and self-acceptance. What "diamond" is keeping you from serenity?

This book started out as a mere dream—a way to chronicle a journey out of the blinding darkness of bipolar mania. I surprisingly discovered *Sham* as I wrote—and how he had taken over my life in 2008. It has been a long haul, with the more recent struggles of dealing with extreme moodiness and mild depressive bouts that caused my psychiatrist to tweak my meds a bit. It was only a few weeks ago that I had the "acronym experience" . . . discovering that self-validation was an important key to my wavering emotional circumstances...that what I needed was to really let go of the need for others to approve of me.

Following our own proclamations can be one of the most difficult things to do, but, with the help of my acronyms and my God, I see myself on this path to fulfillment, this Way of the Lord.

Nietschze wrote:

*Be careful lest, in casting out your devil,*
*you cast out the best thing that's in you.*

I can't (and won't) get rid of *Sham*. Just as I mentioned in an earlier chapter, I see myself as being similar to *Star Trek's* Captain Kirk who needed both opposite parts of himself to be whole. I now realize that *Sham* was really "brought on by" stuffed anger, repressed shame and straggling disappointments. He was destructive—yes—but he was (if you can believe it) doing his best. "His best" was to run, to nearly destroy relationships and to dash my future upon the rocks of uncertainty and certain poverty...financial, social, spiritual.

But, somehow, God saw fit that this inevitability did not occur. I became so ill (as stated in the first paragraph of this book) that I fell apart, and landed in a hospital bed, where I could get help with my bipolar mania. I left a ton of debris behind, relationally and financially, but, well—I'm still here! I have a wife and family who love me and have forgiven me, and bipolar did not get the best of me!!

Lessons I have learned? First, never ignore the fact that I am not sleeping well. This is absolutely crucial to one with this illness. If I would have been more assertive with my psychiatrist a year ago about the fact that I was not getting my sleep, and received more assistance in this area, maybe the fiasco of 2008 would never have occurred.

Second, I now know the feelings that start to arise when I'm not sharing my expectations and frustrations (however meager) with Sandra. I no longer want the feeling of being carried down the river of thoughts that led to *Sham's* intermittent appearances—and his final take-over and ultimate control of my life in August and September of last year. *Sham* is my manic episode in motion. He is not my nemesis, but my unknowingness and my inability to take care of my bipolar symptoms when they arise. *Sham*, although my alter-ego, will never leave me so I'm learning how to feed his hungers with honest open communication with those around me about every aspect of my life. It's either this diligence, or *Sham* may re-appear in even uglier ways in the future. THIS I do not want to happen!

Even though I have ample experience with bipolar mania, I was brought to my knees once more in 2008. Only this time, through meeting the difficulties head on, it eventually created a true understanding of—and respect for—*humility*. It was humility that got me to roll out of that air mattress the night I admitted I had a bipolar problem last October, and humility that allowed me to call Sandra the next day. It was humility that allowed me to come back to Milwaukee in late October, and humility that brought me back to the gospel choir.

The word humility comes from "humus" which means dirt... earth...I have been brought back down to earth by the grace of God and the love of those around me. Now it is time to travel on—into a future of sunshine hope and grounded gratitude. I hope you gained some insight and knowledge, some respect for the illness of bipolar, and some motivation to spread the word that bipolar is NOT a scary monster, but an illness that CAN lead to grace—if only the workings of God are given a chance to grow and bear fruit.

My challenge to you is that you seek to understand your shadow side, in whatever form it may appear. Also, I promote that you seek to form strong connections with your family and friends so that you have a support network established in case bipolar gets out of hand in your life—or the life of a loved one. This network may just be *your* saving grace in times of any future trouble. Travel on—diligently, hope-fully, humbly.

## Connnnnnnnnnnnnnnnnnnnnnections

the bridge from one life
to another is the **connections** noticed
and built upon from the moment we meet another
ccccccc
c
c
c
c
c
**connections** are
the driving force
that attract us, pull us toward one another
be it friendship or love relationship or
just any old interpersonal encounter
j
j
w
w
w
we notice the differences, but *build* relationships
on similarities and commonalities
not superficialities, but curiosities
even the most diverse couple
can discover likenesses in *passion*,
*perception* and *persistence*
that bring the two as close as two atoms
t
t
b
b
b
be aware that your **connections**
with others are the umbilical cord
to your soul as you travel on

your way—they keep you on
the path, and often *create* the path
before you

Thanks for joining me on this path of my authentic journey. Whether you have bipolar, love one with bipolar, or are just now learning about bipolar, may you find peace in your travels.

*Rich Melcher*